THE AUTHOR

BROWNE BARR is minister of
the First Congregational Church in
Berkeley, California.

Dr. Barr was educated at Grinnell College (B.A.), Yale University, and Yale
Divinity School (B.D.). He has held pas-
torates in Middletown and Waterbury
in Connecticut, and in 1953 he succeeded
the late Halford Luccock as professor of
preaching at Yale Divinity School. He
served in this capacity until 1960 when
he accepted his present position in
Berkeley.

In addition to his teaching and pas-
toral duties, Dr. Barr has lectured and
preached in universities and colleges
throughout the United States. He delivered the Lyman Beecher Lectures at
Yale University in the spring of 1963.

EAST BAY
AND EDEN

EAST BAY
AND EDEN

*Sermons on the Drama of Redemption
to a Contemporary Congregation*

BROWNE BARR

ABINGDON PRESS • NEW YORK • NASHVILLE

WW10
B27e

EAST BAY AND EDEN

Copyright © 1963 by Abingdon Press

Library of Congress Catalog Card Number: 63-17824

Scripture quotations unless otherwise noted are
from the Revised Standard Version of the Bible,
copyrighted 1946 and 1952 by the Division of Christian Education, National Council of Churches, and
are used by permission.

Quotations from *The New Testament in
Modern English* by J. B. Phillips are used by
permission of The Macmillan Company.

SET UP, PRINTED, AND BOUND BY THE
PARTHENON PRESS, AT NASHVILLE,
TENNESSEE, UNITED STATES OF AMERICA

For Leigh
who listens and is wise

PREFACE

The title of this volume of sermons is the title of the first sermon, and there is nothing especially original about that. However, *East Bay and Eden* is an appropriate title for the entire book for two important reasons. First, that title suggests the people and the place of the preaching. The reader is invited to bear that in mind as he reads—not that the East Bay is fundamentally different from the Back Bay or the Bay of Fundy or anywhere else, but sermons, unlike essays or novels, come to life in a particular place and among a particular people. The sermon is as much a creation of the people and the place as of the preacher. Indeed, the people who first heard most of these sermons also actually participated in the preparation of some of them and are working every week on more. The scripture is announced a week in advance for study and reflection, and on each Wednesday night members of the congregation who wish to do so come together to hear a brief exegesis of the passage and discuss what it says or fails to say to them. The preacher listens. Often the sermon then takes form as the words of the scripture encounter the people who search them out.

Karl Barth's *Deliverance to the Captives* was published with the actual date when the sermons were preached printed along with the text. So it must be. The timeless gospel is gospel only *in* time and place. Therefore, if the reader will exercise his imagination and come to the East Bay and join the congregation addressed in these sermons as he reads, some of the curse of the printed sermon may be eased. It is for this reason that no effort has been made to alter specific references: San Francisco, Alcatraz, the University of California, the Bay Bridge. To delete all this in an effort to make the sermons universal would have been to destroy them as sermons.

The second reason that *East Bay and Eden* is an appropriate title for the whole volume lies in the word "Eden." This hints at this preacher's conviction that his task is primarily expository. Not all of these sermons are expository, but it is my hope that the faith which they reflect is true to the biblical witness. If "expository" suggests a particularly rigid form or a detailed picking apart of verse upon verse of the Bible, the sermons are not expository. On the other hand, if "expository" means "to open up" the scripture, perhaps some of them may qualify.

Most of these sermons take root and beginning in the Bible, and they conclude with prayer. To omit the prayer fractures the sermon almost more seriously than to omit the scripture. Although most of our preaching fails to reach that high, a sermon should actually feel and be incomplete without the celebration of the Lord's Supper following it. The breaking of the bread should take over and continue the preaching of the Word for which mere words eventually prove inadequate. Despite the widespread failure to follow this practice in Protestant worship, the spontaneous prayer of gratitude after the sermon often bears witness to the inseparability of the exposition of the Word and the Holy Supper. "The Word is not the Word of preaching only," wrote P. T. Forsyth, "it is also the Word of prayer. The Word of all true prayer is stirred by the Word of Grace. It is a function of it. The Eucharist by its very name is much more a thanksgiving than a sacrifice." [1]

The sermons have been arranged to suggest the biblical drama of redemption moving from man's dilemma as a creature to some of the practical consequences of his new creaturehood in Christ. The preacher does not presume that any one of these sermons is a complete or adequate statement of the biblical idea of the Christian doctrine involved. But they do seek to be faithful to these ideas and to suggest that Eden and East Bay are actually much nearer each other than almost anyone in the East Bay believes.

My indebtedness to the congregation which has assisted in the preparation and preaching of these sermons has already been suggested. It is very deep. My indebtedness to many theologians, biblical scholars, and preachers will be evident and, in some instances, explicitly so with or without acknowledgment. Seldom do we know how much of what we present, perhaps *all* we present, is a gift from others which we simply pass on. I hope those who have transmitted so generously to me will understand that recognition of their contribution might inappropriately draw at-

[1] *Congregationalism and Reunion,* Two Lectures in 1917 (London: Independent Press Ltd., 1952).

tention away from it to them. I am, however, eager to express appreciation to my former colleagues on the faculty of the Yale University Divinity School for their stimulation and support, their correction and chastisement, and their own creative work upon which I have so conspicuously leaned.

BROWNE BARR

The First Congregational Church
Berkeley, California
Easter, 1963

CONTENTS

THE CHRISTIAN MAN: HIS LIFE AND LABOR

1
EAST BAY AND EDEN

How far is it from the East Bay to Eden,
from this place and this time where we live to the place and
time where the Lord God formed man from the dust of
the ground and walked in the cool of the day? It is surely
too far for us to care or inquire if we hunt for Eden on a
map or seek to date it in time, if we must lift archaeological
layers or imagine the beginning of every living thing. We
know people who have spent their lives trying to find Eden
and tie it down in history, and thus prove it was real—like
Athens or Jerusalem—and thus have never found it at all.
But the truth is that Eden was in Athens, and the Adam
who walked in Eden walked also in Athens and in Jerusalem
and walks yet on Telegraph Avenue and writes checks to
the power company and works at your desk and sleeps in
your bed. For Adam is everyman, and Eden is every place
and the serpent at his heels and the fruit in his hand and
the woman at his side and the Lord God calling him and
the trees he hides in—these are all the constant and ever-
present dimensions of every life and of my life and of
your life.

East Bay and Eden are always one and the same because we will find in both, if we are sensitive, evidences of the grandeur of man, his Promethean power, his unconquerable greatness, his heroic spirit. There he is, the crown of all creation, dust fanned into life by the very breath of God, rooted in the good earth and yet little lower than the angels who surround the throne of God; master of the soil and of all beasts and bound loyally to the bone of his bones and the flesh of his flesh; rushing into a flaming tenement to save a child unknown by him and breathing in flame and smoke and death, and dying unheralded; subduing the earth and winning dominion over the seas and the skies by the skill of his hands and the diligence of his time and the might of his mind; soaring into space and isolating a virus and telling a child a lovely story at sunset. His image is the image of God with his beauty stretched out like God's on a cross; patience with the sick and faithfulness to the wronged; a strong arm to shelter the weak and a brave voice to defend the oppressed; bravery at Salerno and courage in Jackson, Mississippi. Ah, Adam in Eden and Adam in East Bay—your grandeur is the very image of God, and as he marked you in Eden so does he mark you here with his own greatness, creature of the Creation, and that Creation is good.

But East Bay and Eden are always one and the same because we find in both not only the grandeur of man but the misery of man as well. "In the moving soul there is a frail seam, an old wound, a tender sore. The stout human heart has a wearing ache and a haunting fear." The serpent's voice is heard, and the serpent's voice is heeded. It will not hurt us just this once, you know, and the fruit is taken and tasted—the fruit in Eden—and the sweet, stinking, rosy, rotten, luscious, treasured, malicious word at the coffee break, and it is shared too, so unwilling is man to stand alone in his misery, "and she also gave some to her husband, and he ate." Then the deceit, the lie, the cowardice, the assault, the corrupting, proud act is caught, scratching the grandeur of the image of God, and God marks it out for what it is in his eyes and tracks it down: "Have you eaten," he asks, "have you eaten of the tree of which I commanded you not to eat?" And then it is all doubled and multiplied, and the scar deepened and spread by the design to escape. "The woman whom thou gavest to be with me, she gave me fruit of the tree, and I ate." And as freedom is thus used to mar his greatness, so it is also used to deny his responsibility. But it does not end there, so bound are we in human life, but it is aped and copied in its weakness. And the woman said, "The serpent beguiled me, and I ate." Then the newspaper is out on the street, and the misery of man is sold—a cheat, a whore, a vanity, Buchenwald and graft, and all the perfume of Arabia over the stink, but Duncan is dead.

This is man, this is Adam, mankind, everyman in Eden and East Bay—the unforgettably brave, the majestic moral hero and the splendor of the quiet unsung saint, and the discord and the disease to which he constantly succumbs. This is the paradox of man—man in his grandeur and man in his misery! And every day he is created as he was created in Eden, of the breath of God and of the dust of the ground; and every day he falls as he fell there.

I

The pain of this paradox is in the misery. We would not question life nor contend with the Eden in which we live if the grandeur of man still seemed to have the upper hand, was winning out in the long run over man's misery, if we could still believe, as our fathers did, that the misery of man is petering out, and given a few more centuries and a few more facts and a few more victories, the glory of his original creation would be assured. It was so that our fathers viewed it in the late nineteenth and early twentieth centuries, many of them, heirs of the renaissance, brave optimists! They were to be rid of the fable of the Fall in Eden, that ancient, uncouth, and pessimistic story that no intelligent man would read. Onward and upward! Man was not fallen. He had slipped a little here and there perhaps, and some are weaker than others, to be sure; but all this could be quickly remedied or at least *in time* remedied with an enlightened philosophy freed of the phobias and fears of ancient myths. Many were the tools at hand to liberate man from his miseries and establish him firmly in his grandeur. Evolution, for example, was on his side. His misery, we were told, was the remnant of his animal nature, the tiger or the snake in him; but in time all that would be bred out and leave him purely and grandly man. But the evidence is not encouraging. Some improvement, you know, might be expected in three thousand years or more! And it would be difficult to demonstrate that it has come or will come by natural selection. Others claimed that man's misery stems only from his stupidity and ignorance, and there is large truth in that claim; but if it were the whole truth then the whole cure would be education. This view was held by the Greeks and is yet widely held by us. When we build new churches in our fast-growing suburban areas the educational wing often goes up first and may stand alone for years—a frightening symbol of the confidence that if a choice must be made, it is better to study God than to worship him. This particular Eden east of the Bay is no place to decry the role of education, and a Congregationalist is the last one to do so with Harvard and Wellesley and Dartmouth and Yale and Oberlin and Carleton and Scripps and Pomona and many more—having sprung from the churches of his order. But perhaps especially in this Eden and perhaps especially among Congregationalists, where books are read and teachers are supported, it is better known than elsewhere that "an educated devil is more dangerous than a stupid one."

With evolution and education working to ease man's misery, it ought to be quite eliminated in time and surely hastened if he would just throw in a little more reorganization of society; and there is no doubt that need, too, remains. Yet it has never been made quite clear to me why that need *should* remain if the sinfulness of man is being weeded out by evolution and education. If that is so, why need we stronger laws and more concern for social justice? Should it not work just the other way around? The grandeur of man does not need laws and courts and ordering devices; it is man's misery and sin that call all that into the social fabric. Furthermore, if evolution and education and great cultural and scientific achievements are the instruments by which the misery of man is gradually reduced and his sinfulness made impotent, the history of Germany from 1933 to 1945 is hard to read. Where had culture a more ardent people or education a longer chance?

The mother of Charles William Eliot, who was to be the president of Harvard University and a powerful influence in American education, is reported to have protested to a friend who had joined the Episcopal Church. Recalling the words of the General Confession, she said, "Eliza, do you kneel down in church and call yourself a miserable sinner? Neither I nor any of my family will ever do that!" Well, we who are Mrs. Eliot's descendants, at least not untouched by the mood of her son, may find that phrase still sticks in our throats. We are not yet convinced that *we* are miserable sinners, but is the evidence not now mounting that if *we* are not, other men certainly *are,* and that their sinfulness is contagious? Are we not really worried most of all today about the wickedness of other people and of our own? The grandeur and the misery of man!

II

As this old fact becomes new before our eyes and threatens us with a power multiplied by education and all the advances of our age, we may well look again at Eden and note that the trouble surely cannot be all or even half environmental, for Eden was a cool and lovely place; and it certainly cannot be wholly or even half hereditary, for Adam could not blame his parents! The trouble, you see, was with Adam, with man. Man has sinned and fallen short of the glory of God.

Alas, it may be protested that this is such a gloomy view of man's predicament for such a lovely, sunny day—and in church we need encouragement and comfort and a few minutes' refuge from the storms and stress of life—and how true that is! So why must we be badgered with all this talk about man's misery? "My word, man, I see that in my office and in my classroom and in my shop day by day. Open up, then, some road for us to the grandeur of man." But the roads which are open to us cannot be seen or faithfully followed if we have not marked the blind alleys and put warning lights where the freeway ends unexpectedly. Many cannot take the Church and the gospel which the Church treasures seriously in our time because they have been lured down avenues that lead nowhere. However, the stories of the Creation and the Fall and of Eden and of Adam do encourage us, sustain us, and bring us comfort; but they do so only because, like the Christian faith, they do not blink at the stark ugly facts of human existence, because they do not treat sin as a mere illusion or something that will ultimately work out for good. Our faith takes human nature seriously *both in its grandeur and its misery* and, therefore, is not undone in times like ours when all the Victorian assurances about man and progress and human perfectibility seem increasingly dubious. This ancient story gives us ground for objective, realistic Christian optimism for three clear reasons. Hear them briefly.

III

First, there is ground for optimism because the story of man's fall teaches that the misery of man is not an integral part of his creation. You will note we have the Creation story in chapters one and two of Genesis; we have the Fall in chapter three. They are separated in the Bible, and they are separated in Christian doctrine. The Fall is not part of the Creation, not part of the intrinsic nature of man; and it is introduced not by God into our nature, but by man. It is the result of our rebellion and our disobedience and our strutting desire to be like God. It comes because we are free.

19

It enters human experience not because God created man with his members at war with one another, with evil pounding through his being, but because God made man a free, responsible agent, addressable and responsible, not a puppet or a slave—but man. Be a man! G. K. Chesterton makes this point when he writes, "If I wish to dissuade a man from drinking his tenth whisky and soda, I slap him on the back and say, 'Be a man.' No one who wished to dissuade a crocodile from eating its tenth explorer would slap it on the back and say, 'Be a crocodile'!" If evil were of the essence of man, if it arose from God's intention instead of from man's disobedience, if it were woven into the first and second chapters of Genesis as part of the original creation, then the admonition to be a man would be empty, and our outlook would be the deepest gloom. The Bible does not include sin as part of the image of God in which man is created; nor should we!

The second basis for substantial Christian optimism based on this myth is this: the fact of man's misery is evidence that God has not let go of man. God does not let us get away with the monstrous illusion that man is or can make himself the center of everything. The doctrine of the Fall, far from being a dogma of defeat and a counsel of pessimism, as it has been presented by some of the brilliant theologians in our time, is thus a matter of encouragement. For it proclaims that misery is not man's proper state but rather sure evidence that God still has his hand on man and is trying to rescue him from his own disobedience. He is speaking to man even in his misery. Yea, through his misery—reminding him of his grandeur.

The third support for a far-reaching optimism about man

in the story of the Fall rests in the emphasis on Adam and Eve's sense of shame, "Then the eyes of both were opened, and they knew that they were naked." Man by his sense of shame demonstrates that he yet possesses the nobility and dignity of the image of God. A sense of shame arises only in those who have not altogether forsaken the loveliness and beauty of their original creation. As long as we have the capacity for shame, we may also possess the capacity to respond to God's overtures and remain sensitive to God's love. If this sensitivity had disappeared altogether through man's disobedience, there would be no one—not even we today in this place—with faces turned to God. "For as in Adam all die, so also in Christ shall all be made alive."

Deliver us, O God, from a pessimism which leaves no room for thy power and from an optimism which rests on that which is untrue, but grant that our faith may rest in thee and in acceptance of our redemption as well as our creation. Hear us in Christ's name. Amen.

2

WHY THE HONOR SYSTEM FAILED

TEXT: "In my mind I am God's willing servant, but in my own nature I am bound fast, as I say, to the law of sin and death. It is an agonizing situation, and who on earth can set me free from the clutches of my own sinful nature? I thank God there is a way out through Jesus Christ our Lord." Rom. 7:21-25 (Phillips)

The Boy Scouts line up in the social hall, "On my honor I will do my best to do my duty to God and my country." "On my honor"—this is a promise with one's own esteem, one's own good name offered as security. "On my honor." The examination is over, the blue book filled and on the last page, "On my honor, I have neither given nor received assistance in this examination," with one's name signed, offered again as a seal, a moral promissory note. The young man in the fullness of youth faces his beloved before

22

their friends pledging his honor, "And I do promise and covenant before God and these witnesses to be thy loving and faithful husband in plenty and in want, in joy and in sorrow, in sickness and in health, as long as we both shall live." "On my honor." The candidate for public office circles the town or the county or the state or the nation. "If I am elected, I solemnly promise. . . ." Thus it is that our whole life is permeated with the honor system, promises made by men who offer their own honor as the guarantee of their performance.

Yet the evidence pours in that the performance leaves much to be desired. We have perjured ourselves, we have promised and broken our promises, we have offered our honor and sullied it. The failure of the honor system in our schools is widely admitted. A dozen or more reliable studies of cheating agree in summary that "cheating starts as a technique for getting by in the fifth grade, zooms up in grade eight, erupts again in grade twelve, then, in the college years, perks along among a conservative total of 30 per cent of the students." Every time studies of this sort are made public there is a righteous cry in many quarters as though the breakdown in the honor system were limited to students, but perhaps those students learned long before Boy Scout days to put tongue in cheek or cross their fingers behind their backs when pledging their honor. If so, did they not learn it from parents and counselors who did not really mean "until death do us part," who did not really mean the campaign promise, who were not offended by deliberately misleading advertising, who raised no protest about deceptive packaging of flour and toothpaste? Did these cheaters in grade five and university course 205 learn how cheap honor is even *before* they were

Boy Scouts by parents who told them to tell the caller on the telephone that they were not home when they really were?

When we speak then of the failure of the honor system, we do not refer simply to cheating among students but to the widespread evidence of duplicity and deceit in the relationships of men at every level of life—educational, domestic, commercial, political. The problem is not with our educational system or our domestic arrangements or our commercial life or our political schemes. The problem is man. Cheating in examinations and breaking marital vows and overcharging at the meat counter and compromising in political campaigns are all symptoms of man's deep-seated inclination to seek to serve himself, to make himself and his interests the center of his existence.

The simplest and most interesting and exciting way to deal with all the appalling evidence of cheating and dishonor and immorality is to launch an emotional tirade against it. The press and the pulpit excel in this exercise, and so we are treated from time to time with editorials and sermons and lectures that roar with much noise and eloquence against the soft underbelly of our national life and sweep up purported evidence in art and literature and education, in private and public morals, that our honor system has collapsed. This procedure is widely applauded and enjoyed, but it is dangerous for two reasons. For one thing, we may give ourselves away as we lash out against dishonor of any sort, for it is increasingly evident that we tend to hate in others what we most fear in ourselves. The professional dispensers of smutty books are similar to the promoters of them at least in one particular: they, too, read the books. Our tirade may give us away, but it is dangerous for another reason, too: it doesn't do very

24

much good. Indeed, it may do a great deal of harm because such tirades ordinarily support three dangerously simple presuppositions about human beings and the moral and ethical dilemmas upon which the honor system rests.

I

The honor system in the classroom or culture rests, for example, on the assumption that *any fool can tell right from wrong* if he will just make the effort. The honor system denies the complexity of our ethical and moral decisions, for existence is not like a multiple choice examination with only a few choices with one obviously correct to anyone who has studied his lesson. Our problem may not be to choose between good and evil or even to choose the lesser of two evils but perhaps the lesser of two goods. To be sure, this argument about the complexity of moral decisions can be and is used to rationalize inaction, but that only illustrates the complexity of the problem. A lie is a lie—but will you never lie? Never? Not to save your own life? Good! You are a moral hero in your moral absolutism. But will you never lie not even to save another life? It is wrong to kill; that is clear. But is it right to kill if thereby more killing is thwarted? It is against the honor system to give or to receive assistance in an examination. But is it as wrong to be aware that someone is stealing your work and not report it, as it is to tattle, to report another person when you do not know why he is doing wrong? But then there is the other side to that dilemma, for all society is involved—not just you two. What right have you to be quiet and thus conspire against law and order?

Or again, consider the strong New Testament strictures about divorce. It is difficult to refer to the presumed permanence of the marriage vows in a sermon because in any modern congregation there is a very high percentage of persons who are sorely sensitive at this point: some who have treated those vows shamefully but remained married, and some who have treated them conscientiously and yet been divorced. Who would dare to suggest that it is a simple matter to know what is right and wrong in a sick marriage, who will dare to say that a marriage held together by outward pretense but broken inwardly every day is better than divorce; or who can be sure that if outward unity is somehow sustained, inner unity may not develop? In marriage, as in vocation and in education and in politics, we are confronted with choices that are not black and white, but we must choose between competing values, competing good. To live life at all is to be so confronted, and daily existence is a matter of balancing them. Berdyaev is well heard at this point: "We have pure tragedy when a free personality is confronted with a choice between conflicting values . . . for example, between the value of love and the value of freedom." [1] So many a man in the midst of his moral decisions has learned the meaning and measure of the tragic in life. When we are told, then, that any fool can tell right from wrong if he will only make the effort, we may reply that only a fool believes he commands enough knowledge to claim such comforting certainty about right and wrong.

II

In the second place, the honor system approach rests *on the naïve presupposition that it can succeed without itself being corrupted by pride.* Certainty about right and wrong,

[1] Nicolas Berdyaev, *Destiny of Man* (London: Geoffrey Bles Ltd., 1937), p. 200.

unfortunately characteristic of many reformers and moralists and promoters of simple rules of conduct, leads to the very great evil of Pharisaism—"God, I thank thee that I am not like other men." This is the ever-present peril of the honor system in ethics. If we feel that right and wrong can always be clearly ascertained—that any fool can tell them apart—then we tend to be judgmental and merciless, not only toward evil as we should be, but toward evildoers, forgetting that they are caught in the paradox of moral decisions. When Christian congregations cease to be congregations of people who recognize the moral ambiguities of their existence, who no longer honestly see themselves as sinners in need of forgiveness, when they feel they have nothing to confess and really believe themselves when they say, "I always do the best I know," then they have fallen into this greater evil. This evil forever stalks prosperous churches and rich nations. This moral snobbishness becomes characteristic of people who see religion primarily in terms of social mores, of not smoking or drinking, or in terms of proper ritual and form. It can also easily become characteristic of people who see religion primarily in terms of social reform, race, war, trade, and politics. This second type of Pharisaism may even be more deadly than the first, because any fool *can* indeed see that to abolish racial prejudice or war is more important than to abolish tobacco or promote a particular ritual, and thus the Pharisaism which wears the mask of important rather than trivial concerns is harder to detect in ourselves.

III

There is a third presupposition of the moralists, of the defenders and promoters of the honor system in ethics which we need to consider before we can understand the significance of the New Testament or the Christian religion at all. There are many ways to phrase this presupposition, but in general it has to do with the idea *that any man can raise himself by his own boot straps if he will only make the effort.* It assumes that if a man only knows what is right, he can do it. It may be granted that ethical decisions are complex, that morality is not just black and white, that our choices are often choices between competing and important and positive values, and Pharisaism is an ever-present danger—but granting all that, it is claimed that once a man knows what is right, he can do it.

Is there anyone who has so fooled himself, who is so bandaged from the realities of his own existence that he still believes he possesses the will to do what he knows to be right? Indeed, we so clearly know that we lack the will to do what we know to be right that we comfort ourselves by intellectualizing our moral dilemmas, by going over and over them, nourishing each paradox and consoling one another with the obscurities and difficulties of knowing what is right because we also well know that once we get a clear idea of what is really demanded of us, we will then be face to face with our clear and positive duty as well as our clear and positive inability to do it. The depravity, the corruption, and the distortion of man are focused, you see, in his ability to do, to act, to perform—not only in the mind or the affections. Original sin is not just a matter of being carnally minded, but of having our wrists turn to water when our minds direct our hands into a course of duty which we know to be right.

Could it be that we resist the biblical teaching about man as a mortal, a dependent creature, a sinner, could it be that we are reluctant to admit that it is both difficult to know what is right and more difficult to do what is right because if we once admit all this, we seem to be left in despair? In acknowledging our problem we seem to lose the guide and consolation of our former optimism about ourselves as masters of our fate and captains of our souls, and there is nothing left except to confess dependence on our Maker. If we admit the folly of our optimistic confidence in unaided man, then we seem to have cut the nerve, we think, of effective moral action. If it is really so difficult, as the Bible claims, to know the right and more difficult to do it, then what of us as responsible and moral and ethical creatures? Are we left to wrestle with a nature we cannot master and to exist in a world which seems engaged in a conspiracy to destroy us? That, in fact, is our dilemma, and many persons refuse to face it, refuse to face it not out of stubborn ignorance or moral blindness or religious insensitivity, but because they are wise enough to sense the tragic proportions of the issue here involved and wish to avoid it if they possibly can, as we all wish to avoid the pain of any radical realignment. It is from the midst of this anguish that the great Apostle cries to all generations: "I can will what is right, but I cannot do it. Wretched man that I am! Who will deliver me from this body of death?" And that is the question!

That is the question the Christian faith boldly presumes to answer. Who will deliver us? Who will save us? Deliverer, Saviour, Redeemer. Yet the answer is not heard by those who do not ask the question, and the encouraging word that there is a Saviour falls on deaf ears because we still believe that

29

it is easy to tell right from wrong or that when right and wrong are once settled, it is a simple matter *to do* the right. If that is your experience, then back to the honor system for you; but if that is not your experience, if your daily life is a struggle against a nature that often seems opposed to God and against a backbone that often seems rubbery in doing the small part of God's will you do know, then the Word of a Saviour is relevant. If anxiety about past failures and fears about the future immobilize you in the present so that you can neither trust God nor be a loving person in action toward your neighbor, then the Christian good news is for you. That news is about One who saves us from both anxiety and fear, and thus increasingly frees us to love both God and man in the present, accepting the limitations of our love and wisdom in the unlimited magnitude and mercy of his. In that event, honor systems are not bad; they simply become irrelevant.

O eternal God who hast divided the day from the night and hast sent thy Son to deliver us from darkness and direct us into Light, do thou encourage us through every night and bring us at last into thine everlasting day. Amen.

3

NO PLACE TO HIDE

Text: Ps. 139

"Whither shall I go from thy Spirit? Or whither shall I flee from thy presence?" Most of us have been fed on far too soft a theological diet to hear these words as words of anguish and of anger as they rise from the magnificent 139th Psalm. In this psalm, the crown of the Psalter, the Old Testament reaches the highest conception of the relationship which exists between the individual human soul and God, its Creator. And that relationship is here marked not as one of comfort and peace but of terror and bewilderment as the stumbling, vain, weak man seeks some road of possible escape from the unblinking, unchanging, wakeful eye of Almighty God.

Escape from God? Hide from the Almighty? These questions scarcely bear any meaning, so infused are we with a sentimental religion, a religion of rosebuds and cherubs, a religion of romantic art and easy mottoes, a serviceable religion presided over by an indulgent God who overlooks our sour tempers and to whose ears the cries of the people we have oppressed never reach and whose eyes are closed to our Monday manners; the God of sunshine and Sunday, the God of peace and plenty, the God of opulent Protestantism and prospering Catholicism and secularized Judaism, the God of easy forgiveness and automatic salvation. "Whither shall I go from thy Spirit? Or whither shall I flee from thy presence?" Go? from all that? Flee from such a comfortable One?

Yet, sometimes in the silence of the night or in the midst of prayer or in the presence of some contemporary Amos, we know we have caricatured God. We know that what we sow we *do* reap. We know that there is an unbending moral law which men and nations of men do not finally escape, that justice and wrath and condemnation move in unceasingly upon our soft and accommodating ways. We see our rationalizations in fleeting moments for what they are; we remember our wasted hours and our cowardice and our deafness to human pain, and we know that Judgment Day is real and that Judgment Day is every day, and this day, too. How we loathe these sensitive moments, and how we turn on the people who prompt them and on the situations which expose them, for in them it is we who are exposed. Then in such terrible and frightful moments we begin to understand the cry of the Psalmist. "Whither shall I go from thy Spirit? Or whither shall I flee from thy presence?" Is there, O God, no place to hide from you? No place at all? This is what angered him most, God's pervasive all-seeingness. He was angered and annoyed. God pierced through the excuses and the pretenses. "Even before a word is on my tongue, O Lord, thou knowest it altogether." This invasion of our privacy, this darkness that is as light, as though we hid in center field at Candlestick

Park at three o'clock in the morning and suddenly all the floodlights were turned on. Then hide! Try and hide, O man! And the Psalmist ran and we are running yet—first in one direction and then in another.

I

"If I ascend to heaven. . . ." Hide from God in heaven? Yet, as Paul Tillich reminds us in his brilliant exposition of this Psalm, this is the favorite hiding place for the idealists and the perfectionists of all ages. With our own hands we will build a heaven where everything is lovely, a heaven of our own creation where everything goes well, a tight and regular domestic and professional routine with no room for heavenly visions nor time for heavenly invasions—a well-lined-out career in life where there are no problems, no temptations, no hunger, no strife, no lust, no peril—and thus no need for God. We will beat him at his own game.

This is the promise of the builders of every social Utopia whether they follow the blueprints of Karl Marx or Adam Smith, Khrushchev or the candymaker from Massachusetts; whether they labor for the security of their modern cottage behind a picket fence of protective tariffs and protective missiles or their modern nation shrouded in a Victorian shawl. All this bother about God is nonsense—people will not worry about God anymore when they have all they want here. God is only the comfortable but spurious creation of the weak and the unfortunate who need him to make their miserable lives tolerable. Be miserable no more! Live in heaven! Health, wealth, and an integrated personality—a heaven we can build and there we shall dwell with time to do research on an age that once worried about God.

33

We are thus forever trying one way or another to manipulate our environment to rule out the God who stirs us and judges us. When a man goes from job to job, or from wife to wife, or from town to town, or from cult to cult, we say he is trying to escape from himself—but what is this self from which he seeks to escape? Is he not seeking some Utopia, some heaven, some greener pasture over the fence where the rigorous demands of God to change himself will not be pertinent? But all our heavens are subject to his inescapable terms: selfishness destroys, truth remains, the moral law makes its inevitable arrests.

You know Francis Thompson's poem, *The Hound of Heaven,* which begins, "I fled Him, down the nights and down the days"; and goes on:

I sped;

. . . .

From those strong Feet that followed, followed after.
 But with unhurrying chase,
 And unperturbed pace,
Deliberate speed, majestic instancy,
 They beat—and a Voice beat
 More instant than the Feet—
'All things betray thee, who betrayest Me.'

The Psalmist used fewer words: "If I ascend to heaven, thou art there!"

II

So—turn around and run the other way; surely somewhere there is a hiding shadow—"If I make my bed in Sheol" (if I make my bed in hell). And to the ancient Jew, Sheol or hell was not a place of punishment except in a very subtle sense. It was a vast underground cavern where all memory of God

34

ceased, where there were no moral or religious qualities, or responsibilities or obligations. "If I make my bed in hell" —we will erase the memory of God, separate ourselves from him, destroy everything that reminds us of the days when we believed in him, as the frantic bereaved burn the letters and hide the pictures and rearrange the furniture and avoid the places once shared with the beloved. We will deliberately place ourselves outside with the throngs who are convinced that he is not. We will abandon even the promised comforts of religion to escape the inevitable implications of religious faith.

I cannot speak for others with accuracy, but for myself I can say this is my most steady temptation. There are days when I am sick and tired of the Church and want to separate myself from it, forget it; not because it is faithless and in-effective and weak and isolated and irrelevant, as it often is, but because even in its corruption the Scripture is still read and God's memory held and his Name invoked, and I am weary of being made to feel half-guilty when I am well and prosperous and others are hungry and sick and poor; sick and tired of having an uneasy conscience, weary of the tension which is constantly created when one reads the New Testament and the newspaper side-by-side, worn out by the memory which the Church preserves of a God who expects something rather decent of me for someone besides myself. Much easier, so it seems, if one could be rid of this memory; dwell in hell, separated from it, believing that it is all an illusion. And thus many people in our time embrace such separation with eagerness.

People talk about those silly Christians who believe in the resurrection of the just; such a selfish doctrine it is called.

This I have never been able to understand. It would be far easier not to believe in many ways, not to believe that one day we will meet him face to face, for then we could march along and do as we jolly well please and when the going got too rough just end it all—nothing more, Sheol—the absence of God. It is much easier to live that way than with a memory of the Almighty which makes us take up some part of the world's pain and be responsible for the distended bellies of little children in Asia and to feel a stab when we see someone edge away, especially see ourselves edge away from a neighbor who is difficult or different in color or in status or in ideas.

Yet should we cast our lot with those who would escape God by separation from him, would there not always be the haunting memory of that from which we were separated? Would not our experience in truth be that of the Psalmist; indeed, is it not *that* insofar as we do every day, in a sense, turn our backs and live as though God were not? "If I make my bed in hell, thou art there!" Is there not something of that uncomfortable and wistful memory which drives so many people to church at Christmas and Easter and keeps some talk of God—some polite courtesy to him in our public functions—his Name on our coins even when we use them to buy a ticket to hell?

III

If I ascend to heaven—he is there; if I make my bed in hell, he is there too. So next the Psalmist anticipates, not only the spirit, but the determination of our century: "If I take the wings of the morning and dwell in the uttermost parts of the sea." "The wings of the dawn," so it may be translated, and what a beautiful phrase, occurring this single time in the whole Bible—"the wings of the dawn," beautiful and tempting. Don't bother about the new and difficult sociological and moral problems of a world drawn into one intimate neighborhood; take the wings of the dawn and conquer the moon, fleeing once more from the demands of God on his people. Don't bother about the call for righteousness and for justice. Ignore the demands that call all your time and effort and money into the pressing questions of fair play and brotherhood and food and peace. Stay close to your laboratory— there are scholarships a plenty for that so we can beat the Russians to the moon!

Yet how dramatically the Psalmist's discovery is being confirmed among us in our time that even with the wings of the dawn there is no place to hide. "If I take the wings of the morning and dwell in the uttermost parts of the sea; even *there* thy hand shall lead me, and thy right hand shall hold me." It may be a pious fiction elsewhere, and it is certainly a popular one, but it is true in this parish in my experience here, that it is the men of science who are most worried and who speak the most indignantly of those who pin their hopes for a world of peace on pushing back the frontiers of space. The inescapable God, his Word is universal: hatred breeds hatred and destroys him who hates; self-interest cankers the inner life of a man and of a nation; distrust and suspicion corrode. All this does not change, and we cannot hide, not in heaven or in hell or in the uttermost parts of the sea!

For me there is no surer mark that all this is pressing truth than in my own reluctance to pray, a reluctance most strong with me and perhaps it is with you when I wish the most desperately to hide from God, to live as though he were not and to manage my own affairs without his infernal interference. But by prayer I do not mean just a formal thing but an opening up of life to his constant presence, centering life in communion with him, falling down before him in such profound worship that all the lesser gods we count on are seen in their proper and miserable perspective. Yet that is so difficult—so difficult that I dare guess even now there are many of us saying, "Well, this is just a pat and pious answer to grave problems." But if life centered in faith and prayer is difficult, how can we manage it? There is no other way except to face the Almighty and wrestle with him and be torn and tossed by his stern and creative discipline. For have we not learned this much from our common life, that the best fashion to meet a problem is head on?

Have you ever had some alienation and then have you put off settlement of it and sought to evade it and trusted that somehow it would work out in time? Then for some reason you were compelled to face it forthrightly and learned to your delighted surprise that this is the only way it is cleared. Or have you had a falling-out with a friend, and that bitter edge of life grew worse and worse until you met him one day face-to-face and acknowledged the situation and then there was some ground for reconciliation.

Perhaps in the tumult of our day God is trying to shake us up and turn us back to him, face-to-face, for certainly there is no other way to handle our constant flight. The chase ends in Thompson's poem:

> Halts by me that footfall:
> Is my gloom, after all,
> Shade of His hand, outstretched caressingly?

'Ah, fondest, blindest, weakest,
I am He Whom thou seekest!'

And so this magnificent psalm, too, ends with one of the great prayers of the Bible: "Search me, O God, and know my heart! Try me and know my thoughts! And see if there be any wicked way in me, and lead me in the way everlasting!" Here is the only possible resolve of our dilemma. From that which is inescapable there is no relief save in the honest facing, and we are made bold to do so because the insistence we cannot escape has been revealed in Jesus Christ our Lord, and it is not the insistence of a tyrant's wrath but the insistence of a Father's love.

Search us, O Lord, and know our hearts! Try us and know our thoughts! And see if there be any wicked way in us, and lead us in the way everlasting! Through Jesus Christ, our Lord. Amen.

4

THE THIRD THIEF ON GOLGOTHA

> TEXT: "For you yourselves know well that
> the day of the Lord will come like
> a thief in the night." I Thess. 5:2

Today we have followed a September cus-
tom in this congregation and have sung the hymns of the
University of California and the Pacific School of Religion.
To do so celebrates not only the pride which Congregationalists feel for the crucial role of their fathers in the founding
of both of these schools and the continuing concern of this
church for their welfare, but it also indicates our eagerness
to welcome here students, new and old, from all the schools
in this area. We welcome this contemporary generation with
many opportunities: here is the new student center building
made possible, not by the gift of one wealthy man or founda-
tion, but by the sacrifice of scores of ordinary people in this
parish; here is the ministry of the church with special train-
ing for meeting persons in the tempest of college years; here
is the warmth of a concerned and friendly congregation determined that no one among us, young or old, Phi Bete or

playboy, shall feel friendless or alone in any circumstance of life! Here then is this parish church offering such opportunity that it might fittingly erect a statue of liberty outside its doors with a flaming torch rising loftily above and a noble inscription below:

> Send these, the homeless, tempest-tossed to me:
> I lift my lamp beside the golden door.

However, all this sounds more like Madison Avenue advertising copy than it does like the New Testament. A careful reading of the New Testament does not disclose that the mission of the Church is to win people to an institution or to provide the comfort of a plush lounge or to insulate them against the storms of life whether in the old Athens of Greece or the new Athens of California. Rather the mission of the Church is to confront people, young and old, rich and poor, bright and dull, with the risen and living Lord. The symbol among us is not the flaming torch in the New York harbor but this empty cross on Golgotha. The meaning of our services rests not in gathering a warm middle-class mutual admiration society sparked with just enough aesthetic and intellectual sophistication to win the interest of warm middle-class students; rather the meaning of our service rests wholly in the belief that there is a vertical dimension to life running between the Creator God and his creatures and that the preaching of the Word, the reading of the Scripture, the administration of the Sacraments, the singing of the hymns and anthems, and the mutual support of one another in love are all instruments, channels, vehicles for our confrontation with the Word, the Nature, the Will, the Being of Almighty God. Casting all other concerns aside, spurning all other attractions, the awe-full burden of the Church is to make each Lord's day the day of the Lord, where the humdrum of the hours is split open and enlivened by an invasion of the eternal. So we sing, "Come, Lord Jesus, dwell with me."

However, if you remember that gospel song, you will recall that the tune is sentimental and the tone saccharine. It may then be a shock to hear our text: "For you yourselves know well that the day of the Lord will come like a thief in the night." Biblical scholars may be quick to remind us that the phrase "the day of the Lord" in this text refers primarily to the expectation of the early Church that their Lord would soon return to establish his kingdom, to divide the sheep from the goats, to set things right—the Second Coming. Nonetheless, it is not mystical double-talk or theological jargon to affirm the truth that whenever the perfect love which was in Christ confronts a man either in personal or public history, either in the midst of life's day or at the end of all history, there is, in truth, a Second Coming—a day of the Lord, and that day, so our text claims, comes like a thief in the night.

It may offend our sensibilities to compare the day of the Lord to a thief, much less to compare our Lord himself to a thief, but the biblical writers were not so inhibited. The writer of Revelation hears Jesus saying, "I will come like a thief," and it has been pertinently suggested that there were really three thieves, not two, on Golgotha. Thus Paul Minear reminds us that the New Testament writers "did not hesitate to speak of Christ as a robber." [1] If our Lord comes as a thief, his coming scarcely appears to be an attraction for

[1] *Christian Hope and the Second Coming* (Philadelphia: The Westminster Press, 1954).

the Church to advertise as she seeks to win friends and influence people. But how is the coming of Christ like the coming of a robber? Let us mark three ways.

I

In the first place when Christ invades human life, he robs us of our accustomed security. When I was a child, my parents left me in the care of a trusted nursemaid while they took a holiday in sunny California. One night during their absence the nursemaid awoke to see a burglar standing in the bedroom we shared. As she shrieked, he fled with her pocketbook. The nursemaid, long a member of our household, from that night to the night she died many years later could never stay alone in a house at night. The security of locks and keys, of doors and walls, was shattered for her.

We rest thus, many of us, in the comfort of a temporal security which Christ, if admitted, destroys. Kierkegaard puts it thus: "He did not steal the money of the rich—no, but he took away the estimation from human honor and reputation." As a nation have we not rested, at least until lately, in our sense of superiority; have we not felt secure in the knowledge of our advanced laboratories and widespread literacy and our immense national wealth? But Christ comes taking all that away not by appropriating it, but by devaluating it, revealing its ultimate weakness, like the weakness of Rome. During the last war Maud Royden of England shocked many people by saying, "If this war had not occurred, I would have found it hard to believe in God." Christ thus destroys our outward security, saying in effect: You people want peace, but you fulfill all the conditions for war; you encounter immature frantic behavior at Paris and you respond with immature frantic behavior in Washington; you praise the power of truth but find your security in its suppression. You American Protestants find your treasure in your avowed superiority of origin, of history, of education, of class, of wealth, but these treasures moth and rust destroy and thieves break through and steal—and these treasures, if you meet me as you claim in your services, I, too, will destroy by drastic re-evaluation: the standard is changed and the security gone. "Come, Lord Jesus, dwell with me. . . ." But when he comes, the old security evaporates. If we open our safe-deposit boxes and finger the jewels and bonds and contracts in his presence, they seem to turn to dust in that Light.

Not only does he steal away our outward security, but he also robs us of our inward security. One of the most popular and devastating heresies in Protestant circles today is the crass contention that Christ gives us peace of mind. So we build our churches like great plush theatres with upholstered folding seats and a rheostat to dim the lights and create a "religious" atmosphere and all but provide couches for the redeemed to rest on while they listen to some encouraging advice. Peace of mind, my word! How can we have peace of mind when we even faintly hear his holy Word or with a clear eye measure the costliness of his love? Why do we so seldom hear these texts: "I came not to send peace, but a sword"; "With what judgment ye judge, ye shall be judged"; "Enter ye in at the strait gate"; "Not everyone that saith unto me, Lord, Lord, shall enter the kingdom of heaven"? This New Testament is scarcely a manual on inner peace but rather one on inner tension—the sort of tension which is creative and constructive and brings forth the new man out of the old.

To be sure, we appreciate the truly stable personality, but often the level of our stability is at the lowest possible understanding of our creation and our destiny. So very little troubles us if we are well-housed and well-fed. To possess casual peace of mind in our generation is a sure mark of indifference and insensitivity, of failure to be a full and responsible human being living life at its dangerous exciting vital center. Christ robs us of every inward security which depends upon easy answers to the hard knotty questions of human existence.

II

In the second place (and note how surely this follows the first) *an encounter with Christ is like an encounter with a thief because our spontaneous reaction is one of anger and of fear.* Certainly if he strips from us traditional securities, as we have contended, we will react with anger and fear as a child rebels when he is separated from his comforting blanket or teddy bear. When in some casual conversation a comment provokes a heated flashing response, we sense at once that we have unintentionally hit a sore point. We may warn others later, "Be careful, he's very touchy on that subject." People thus respond who are threatened, as a thief threatens.

Thus we who lose our lives in our livelihood, like the man who built more and more barns to store his goods, do not welcome him who devaluates our livelihood. We rationalize his claims; we assert the final dictum of practicality, for we have been hit at a sore point. So is the universal response of the natural man, the man centered in self, when he senses the demand of a God who loves to the uttermost.

Within three blocks of this church there is a semi-public

place with the most hateful sort of obscenities against Christ and the Church scratched on the wall, a foul mark left there by some angry person. He may have been possessed by a justified anger: perhaps he had seen the Church socially exclusive, accommodating itself to its culture, making no bold thrusts at transforming it. There are distressingly many reasons for a sensitive man to be righteously angry with the Church—but *righteously* angry with Christ, no! Our anger there is not apt to be righteous anger but the anger of fearful men who feel themselves judged, threatened—the anger of a profound fear. I often suspect that many acute and perceptive persons stay clear of the church not because the church is full of weakness and sham and hypocrisy, as indeed it is, but because they know that it may be for them a meeting place, a skirmish with him who is the great disturber of man. And their anger with the church is not so much the anger of the righteous as the anger of the threatened. So Studdert-Kennedy puts it in cockney rhyme:

> There ain't no throne, and there ain't no books,
> It's 'Im you've got to see,
> It's 'Im, just 'Im, that is the Judge
> Of blokes like you and me.
>
> And, boys, I'd sooner frizzle up,
> I' the flames of a burnin' 'Ell,
> Than stand and look into 'Is face,
> And 'ear 'Is voice say—"Well?" [2]

[2] "Well?" From the Unutterable Beauty, p. 141, by G. A. Studdert-Kennedy. Copyright by Harper & Row, publishers, Incorporated. Reprinted by permission.

III

In the third place the coming of Christ is like the coming of a thief in the night because he comes suddenly, when we least expect him. My timid nursemaid looked up one night and saw the burglar prowling through her room seeking her wealth; uninvited and unexpected he came, and with great suddenness. Our thinking is so framed by evolutionary doctrine, so accustomed to the truth of slow gradual growth and slow gradual decay, almost imperceptible change, that we often fail to recognize that human experience has its moments of crisis, the great watershed, a final divide. The word "crisis" comes from the Greek "to reveal" or "to disclose," and in these moments of crisis much is revealed about us, a spontaneous response which announces our character.

Early one Sunday morning last winter while the streets were still deserted, I drove past a house and could not believe what I saw, and then quickly it was clear. Not only was that house on fire, but apparently I alone knew it. There I sat in my stopped car—a sudden, unexpected crisis—preparing to disclose something about me. Fortunately I escaped that judgment, for spreading the alarm proved to involve no great risk, but in a split second I was confronted with a crisis, which, had it been slightly different, would have revealed much about me. In that moment Christ came, if you will, suddenly like a thief in the night, making his imperial demands, the demand of love and purpose and honor, the demand of compassion and courage. So he does come to us all, deny it as we will; suddenly, in the midst of our experience, there is a moment of decision, of crisis, of reaction, of

47

response—unavoidable, where failure to respond is response itself, and failure to decide is decision itself.

It is recorded that Studdert-Kennedy, who wrote the cockney rhyme, told of a single experience in the first World War when he stumbled over the dead body of a German, a mere boy, and as he looked and thought, the boy seemed to disappear, and in his place lay Christ upon the Cross. Years later, near the end of his courageous life, Studdert-Kennedy is reported to have said that from that moment on he never saw a battlefield as anything but a crucifix and that in every slum, in every filthy over-crowded quarter, he saw the Cross established. From that day to the day he died, it was Christ on his Cross that stared at him from every newspaper telling of a tortured, lost, bewildered world, calling all brave men and women to share his sorrow and help save the world. A man's life sent in a powerful new direction when, staring out from a small fragment of the tragedy of mankind, that man saw Christ.

Perhaps there is some person here today who has come to find God. "There is a good deal in the Bible about men seeking God," as D. M. Baillie reminds us, "but there is much more about God seeking men, and coming upon them unawares when they were not seeking Him" [3]—yea, more! when they were fleeing from him just as fast as they could. You see, God is not lost that we must search for him. It is we who are lost and God who is persistent in his search, and the night, the darkness, in which he comes, is our night, not his. See the third thief on Golgotha, the Divine Robber, who takes from us our accustomed security, provokes our anger and fear, steals in upon us suddenly—becomes a thief in the night, in

[3] *God Was in Christ*, (New York: Charles Scribner's Sons, 1948), p. 64.

any way to get through to us to find us that he might save us, that having been emptied, we might be filled with all the fullness of God.

O thou from whose Spirit we do seek in vain to flee, steal thou into our days and into our nights leading us by thy hand and upholding us with thy love in Christ, our Saviour. Amen.

5
AND DWELT AMONG US

> TEXT: "And the Word became flesh and dwelt among us, full of grace and truth." John 1:14

This is the central and incredible claim of the Christian faith—that the Almighty and Everlasting God robed himself in human flesh and dwelt among us, "pleased as man with men to dwell." Our immediate response to this claim, especially if we are untempered by time or untouched by tragedy, is to ask, "Is it true?" And then follow in unseemly train all the disputes and arguments about the divinity of Christ, the Virgin Birth, the truth of scripture, and the precise meaning of the creed. See the vigor and speed with which we then wrap ourselves up in controversy and intellectual gymnastics! However, there is within me a deep suspicion that our immediate response to this incredible announcement is not really the question of its truth. Was God really in Christ? Arguing that question may only be a screen we throw up to hide our deeper and more spontaneous reaction. Do you remember rushing out to your playmates one day when you were a child to tell them that your favorite uncle was coming for a visit? You were full of the "good news" because you knew what it meant. Perhaps he was a rich bachelor and always brought you extravagant gifts. As you eagerly told your friends about his coming, their response was not "Is it true?" but in all likelihood they grunted, "Well, so what? What difference does it make to us?" Is it not thus with the Christian "good news" of the Incarnation that God was in Christ, that the Word became flesh? So what? What personal practical difference does it make to us here and now?

I

Well, if it is true God was in Christ, it makes more difference than words can describe, but today mark these two: First, if God became man, that action, that becoming, says something about man, about you and me. It puts us in the first ranks of creation; it declares the lofty possibilities of human nature. Surely in our time no sane person questions man's capacity for evil. In this connection a student reminded me of the final scene in the play *The Desperate Hours*. Escaped convicts take over a middle-class suburban home in Columbus, Ohio. An ordinary man and his wife and two children are held in terrorized captivity through many desperate hours. In a final scene, the young son of the household, a lad of twelve years, is roughly held as a shield by one of the bandits. There is a gun in the lad's back and cursing and threats in his ears. All the evil of the convict's frightening face and twisted person reaches out and entwines the boy and makes him weak and afraid, afraid to pull himself free and run to his father who stands across the room. In that moment, the child is enthralled, held captive if you will by the power of the evil in the bandit's bleary eyes and unsteady hand.

That boy's dilemma is ours: we, too, are held back from our Father's arms and thus enthralled by love of self, and corrupted by our alienation from him; we push and haul and lie and steal for our little place in the sun. Every parking ticket, every lock and key, every contract with dotted line bears witness to the weakness and corruption of human nature. The doctrine of the depravity of man would not offend us if we did not quietly sense its truth; the insults which trouble us and make us bristle are not the ones obviously ridiculous but the ones etched with some truth we cannot quite acknowledge. Man *is* deeply twisted, a fallen angel with face turned from God, yet despite all that, God chose, so the Christian faith proclaims, to reveal himself through a man. Why? The answer leaps at us: there were no more adequate means. Why not through a star or in magic writing in the sky; but a star cannot weep and suffer and die for us, and magic writing in the sky cannot stoop and lift our burden and love us. But a man can, a human being can, if he will. The Incarnation, the coming of God in Christ, forever reminds us of the lofty possibilities in the most unpromising man: an angel, fallen to be sure, but still an angel. We have within us the capacity not only to become Storm Troopers, fools, bigots, weaklings, bullies; but by God's grace we may become angels of mercy, heroic defenders of truth, gentle obscure saints stubbornly and defiantly holding aloft in dark days a steady light. Let no sound doctrine of sin obscure that truth!

II

If it is true then that God was in Christ, we can mark this first practical personal difference which it makes to us: it underscores our potentialities for good. But if that is the only difference it makes, we will surely be left worse off than when we began, so far do we stand from any such goodness, so steady and consistent is our failure. But that is not all. It makes this second difference: the faith that God was in Christ tells us something also about God. It tells us that if God were made flesh, that if God were in Jesus, a human person, then God is somehow person. That is, he possesses at least the attributes of personality. He is not just First Cause, the force that started everything rolling, not just a power working for righteousness or anything else. He is Person. The word Person constantly occurs in every Christian discussion of God, but oft used, it slips smoothly past us without our recognition of the very least it means, and that very least is this: that God is not less than the best we have ever encountered in human personality. Have you ever noticed how often we fail to credit God with having even as much sense as we have, much less as much compassion or wisdom? Or we make him so remote that we really think of him as being someone "subhuman"? It is dangerous to get cozy with God. He is high and lifted up and beyond our searching, but if we had to make a choice, I suspect we would be nearer to truth to think of him as an old, wise, kindly man with a long white beard than to think of him as a mysterious abstract breeze spirit that gently stirs the highest treetops. But we are not left to any such unhappy and inadequate choice. God has shown himself to us as person, that whatever more he is, he possesses the powers, the gifts, the feelings of personality. He, too, is

grieved and pained; he is joyous and glad; he possesses feelings—see Jesus of Nazareth—and possesses them in such
beauty and splendor and perfection that the best we have
known in human life is but a dim and broken reflection of
him.

III

But you may fairly be thinking still, "So what? What difference does it make if on the one hand human nature possesses lofty possibilities, and on the other God possesses the
attributes of personality?" The difference will only be readily
apparent if you are a serious-minded person who is stirred
by his lofty possibilities but who is also aware of the gap between his intentions and his actions, who has before him
standards of integrity and honor which he repeatedly vio-
lates: for it makes a difference to every man with any sense
of regret or remorse or guilt in his life. We may bravely deny
any sense of guilt but our bravado gives us away. As long as
the words "duty" and "liability" and "obligation" are on
our tongues, there will be guilt in our souls. Every *simple*
panacea offered to help us deal with it strengthens its deadly
hand. "Leave home," "forget it," "think positively," "keep
busy," "try harder"—all these only thrust it more deeply
within us to do its deadly work. The only lasting help is in
confession to one who can really forgive and the subsequent
liberating sense of forgiveness. Unconfessed, our guilt is (un-
consciously) repressed and "becomes a morbid complex with
paralyzing effects." [1] But to *whom* shall we confess? We can
only receive forgiveness from the one we have offended. Shall

[1] D. M. Baillie, *God Was in Christ* (New York: Charles Scribner's Sons,
1948).

we then run around the neighborhood and find everyone we have ever slandered or cheated? That would be quite an undertaking—and sheer nonsense. Of course, we should make such restitution as we can. If we are at odds with our neighbor, we should go to him and set things straight in so far as we are able. But, alas, who is our neighbor, and how far do our wrongs march? You abused a man five years ago, and he is now dead and cannot be reached to hear your confession and offer forgiveness. Perhaps you never knew his name —a stranger in some black night. And you do not know, you cannot know, all the avenues down through which that wrong has moved or all the involvement of others in pain or infidelity which it has caused or may yet cause in someone not yet born. But the dead cannot forgive, nor can the unborn forgive, and both are involved in our sin so inextricably bound in human life. And no one can act as their proxy either, for only the one who is offended can forgive. The psychiatrist cannot say, "You are forgiven, go in peace," unless in some rare instance he is the only one involved—and that rare instance never occurs, because our offense is always and forever against this whole indivisible creation, against, you see, the Creator himself. It is not only some moral law we violate when we lie; we violate God who is Truth. It is not our own self-erected standard we hack at when we reach out and greedily pull good things to ourselves while others shiver and starve; we hack at God who is compassion. It is not simply our own sense of honor we disobey when we ride the fence mugwump fashion on the crucial issues of our day; we disobey God from whom all beauty flows, who is the wellspring of integrity and love, of courage and honor.

Alas, our transgressions are more serious than we have

imagined. They are not private little vices or grave public crimes which we can clean up in an afternoon's confessional tour around the neighborhood or by thirty years in jail, but assaults on the very being of God, assaults pounding furiously through the generations and at the very gate of heaven. The final ultimate power of life is offended and if that final power is only moral law, sad is our plight, for law cannot forgive. If that ultimate power is only a power working for righteousness like electricity, unseen but potent, we are surely in desperate straits, for sheer power is impersonal. There is no going home again to it. Such is our dilemma if God be not Person. We are trapped by our own weakness, suffocated by our burden of guilt. But here is the tremendous personal, yes, practical difference which it makes if in truth "the Word became flesh," for in Christ we are confronted not only by a very good and brave and selfless man, but by a God who by his very nature could penetrate human flesh; and finding him here, we find him personal, able and willing and eager to lift from us the crushing burden of our incompleteness, our weakness, our guilt, gathering it all up into himself once and for all, yet ever and again upon the cross and giving us the grace of a fresh beginning every day.

IV

When we once sense that it means all this and more to us personally, directly, immediately, if God was in Christ, the question "But is it true?" presses forward not with casual academic curiosity, but with the urgency born of hope. Well, is it true? Do we find in him a Person who forgives and renews, who reconciles and saves? Each man must find his own answer. But it is not found in sermon or textbook or argument; it is found only through a bold thrust of confidence and dependence, of faith—moving over to the final security of the arms of him who loves us and has given himself for us. Faith is not simply to believe that God *is* as we believe in the existence of some person we have only heard about; but faith is to believe *in* God as we believe in a friend who has been faithful to us even when we have disappointed him.

The boy who was separated from his father and held by the escaped convict in *The Desperate Hours*,[2] hopelessly ensnarled in his will and bound by the might of his gun, did not know one vital truth about his situation. Some hours before, his father had managed to get at the two guns that the bandit had and to unload one and take the other. The father stood now across the room with the loaded gun; the bandit held the lad as shield with the unloaded gun. The father alone knew it was not loaded and that everything would be all right if the lad would pull loose from his captor.

"Ralph . . . listen to me," he implored the boy, "that man is not going to hurt you."

"Try budgin', kid, and you'll find out," the convict snarled.

"Ralph . . . have I ever lied to you?" the father replied. "Now—I want you to do exactly as I tell you. Because that gun is not loaded."

The bandit pressed the cold unloaded gun into the lad's back and twisted his arm tighter still.

"It has no bullets in it, Ralph," the father persisted. "Do you understand that?" Then he stepped aside slightly to clear the way and shouted to the boy, "Run!" In a rush of faith the lad plunged across the room into his father's arms as the

---

[2] Quoted material from the play, *The Desperate Hours,* by Joseph Hayes, has been paraphrased with permission of Random House, Inc. (1955).

bandit's gun clicked uselessly without power to enslave any
longer. Such is the promise of Christ: "And him that cometh
to me I will in no wise cast out."

*O thou, who knowest our hearts and weakness, forgive us
our much talk and open us so to receive thy Holy Spirit
that we may believe in thee and trust thee and find refreshment and strength at thy side. Amen.*

6
NO DISTANT THRONE

TEXT: Let us then with confidence draw
near to the throne of grace, that we
may receive mercy and find grace to
help in time of need. Heb. 4:16

It is rough, isn't it, this life we share? The
whole world is rocking, teetering back and forth on the line
between East and West, sliding this way and that. We reach
out to hold on to something, and it breaks loose like a door
knob with the setscrew lost. We fall and pick ourselves up
and brush ourselves off only to be pitched into another crazy
lurch: Berlin, bombs, shelters, summits, intrigue, threats,
common market, new market, no market at all; the whole
world, the vast outward scene of our life groaning and
travailing together! But a man can face up to all that, take
it all in his stride, if there is a safe and quiet place in the
smaller scene of his own personal domain carefully marked
out and controlled; but that is rough, too, painful beyond acknowledgment for scores of folk with no shelter, for youth

breaking into maturity, perplexed and frightened with a pretended bravado, or for the aged breaking into eternity perplexed and frightened with a pretended resignation, or for the middle-aged expected to be wise and rich and strong and knowing himself to be ignorant and poor and weak. Peel off the veneer of poise and order and the pitiful truth breaks out: the truth of loneliness and bewilderment, the truth of pain over our children or our childlessness, the truth of our unending disappointment and our failure of nerve and weakness of will.

Small wonder then that a person of apparent sensitivity and honesty asks, "Do you really believe in a God who cares for persons, who is really concerned with individuals?" That is THE question, isn't it? We can spend our eloquence extolling God, the creative force, the final sum of all our celestial and terrestrial arithmetic, the power enthroned above and behind the most distant mystery. Indeed, we can well-nigh compel assent to belief in some such power by the logic of the classical arguments for the existence of God; but scant difference all that eloquence and all that persuasion make when a man stands in the brokenness of his own days with the demand for courage stretching him out in strained agony to get a handhold on life. We can believe in this great cosmic impersonal God, agree that there is too much order and beauty and law in creation for it to have come about by accident and still, for all that, have no God, not one whose throne we can draw near, not one from whom we may receive mercy and find grace to help in time of need. If the only God we believe in occupies a distant throne and is unknowable and unapproachable, we are for all practical purposes atheists. This is the practical atheism which David Roberts claimed each one of us carries around in his heart much of the time, a practical atheism "far more to be dreaded than the pallid skepticism of intellectuals in the classroom." [1]

I

It is this practical atheism which leaves us in a frozen state of spiritual isolation, cut off from any source of help or meaning beyond ourselves. Our lives *are* rough—the recital of our pain and fear and perplexity is not empty rhetoric. Meet your neighbor at some deeper level than the banalities of social convention, meet him with the compassion and tenderness you sorely yearn for yourself, and you will find it true— our lives are rough; but it is not the roughness that makes them barren and frightening and meaningless, but the sense of isolation and separation from him who brought us and all that is into being. "He that dwelleth in the secret place of the most High shall abide under the shadow of the Almighty." "The Lord is my shepherd; I shall not want." "The very hairs of your head are all numbered." O my God, do you really know me and hold me in the shadow of your hand! Such inner conviction, such pervasive and personal trust is the clearest need of countless men and women in our frantic age; furthermore, it is a need which Christian faith promises to meet—yet how many of us feel it is the need most unmet in our lives, a promise unfulfilled for us.

The preacher's temptation is to try to deal with this prob-

[1] *The Grandeur and Misery of Man* (New York: Oxford University Press, 1955).

lem at the intellectual level—and there are serious intellectual obstacles to such faith. The modern church must with candor and clarity provide the opportunity and the atmosphere for people to deal with such questions rigorously and persistently. But even more, the modern church must help people find their weary way to the throne of grace itself—not simply describe it or argue about it or get lost in the defense of it.

If the church is to fulfill that task, then it must never forget that it is the Church of Jesus Christ and not a vague religious society with no special treasure or mission; it must remember and proclaim the essence of the gospel it possesses, the good news that God does care for persons, and that the road to his gracious throne has been opened up for all men through the life and death and resurrection of Jesus Christ. The text exhorts us, "Let us then with confidence draw near to the throne of grace." But it is this *confidence* to draw near we lack, and we lack it at two crucial points, one on the *Godward side* and one on the *manward side*. It is precisely at these two points that Christ inspires our confidence, removes the barriers, opens the way.

II

On the *Godward side* our confidence in approaching the throne of grace is shaken because the nature of God is obscured, hidden from our eyes. We cannot see God face to face; how can we trust him? His throne is veiled. How dare we approach it? When we are held back from his presence because of the veil which hides him from our eyes, we stand where the pious Jew did in Jesus' time. He worshiped, as

James Stewart of Edinburgh reminds us, in a temple where

a massive curtain hung before the inmost shrine. . . . It was there to fulfill a double function. On the one hand, it was there to keep men out. . . . On the other hand it was there to shut God in; for behind that hanging veil there was silence deep as death and darkness black as night even while the sun was blazing outside. It had been hanging there for years: it looked as if it might hang there forever.[2]

God had been dealing with his people through the centuries; he had engaged them in solemn covenant; he had given them the Promise and the Law; he had sent his prophets and teachers; he had at long last sent Jesus Christ, "appealing to men in tones they had never heard before to trust God's love for everything . . . but the veil of doubt still lingered," the throne of grace was still shrouded in mystery, and the curtain still hung in the temple marking the final mystery that the mind of man could not pierce, the mystery of the absent God. Then one day Jesus was crucified, rejected, and despised by men, but loving them yet and obedient unto death, even the death of the cross—and in that death, in that divine action, everything changed. When the Gospel writers tried to tell of it and what it meant and what they now knew with confidence as a result of that death, they recorded it: "And Jesus cried again with a loud voice and yielded up his spirit. And behold, the curtain of the temple was torn in two, from top to bottom." The nature of God was exposed by God himself in a saving act, an act of absolute love, an event in history, the Word made flesh—"we have beheld his glory, glory as of the only Son from the Father." Two thousand

[2] *A Faith to Proclaim*, (London: Hodder and Stoughton, 1953), p. 80.

years later Winston Churchill addressed the men at Massachusetts Institute of Technology and spoke as Christians have
ever since of the blessings of a *revealed* religion, and the fore-
most of those blessings is this: that we need no longer wonder
about the nature of God. The death of Christ has ripped
from top to bottom the veil from the throne of God. So Paul:
"Whom therefore ye ignorantly worship, him declare I unto
you." This is the work of Christ on the Godward side, revealing to us in his life and in his death "the image of God.
Because God is invisible and cannot be seen by us in this
life," writes Canon Richardson, "we can think about him
only in images; and Jesus Christ is the final image and the
great glory."

III

"Let us then with confidence draw near to the throne of
grace," it is no longer veiled; we have seen Jesus, we acknowledge his revelation of God; we can call him Lord—but
yet we are hindered, held back, we do not draw near, our
confidence is shaken now not from the Godward side, but
from the *manward side*. The veil is not now over the face of
God, but over our faces. How can we presume to enter the
presence of one so utterly holy; we have a new and higher
and stunning sense of the greatness of God. "Woe is me!"
cried Isaiah, "for I am a man of unclean lips, and I dwell
in the midst of a people of unclean lips."

The final barrier confronting even the devout is not the
problem of God's holiness or goodness, but doubt that such
a god could know one so stained and small as he. It is genuine
humility that holds us back, as a modest man hesitates to

press his friendship on a famous man he knew long ago. What could God have to do with me? Does he not dwell in light unapproachable, and I in the gray darkness of finite man? His throne is in the palace beyond all the palaces of all the kings of all the empires, so our inadequate images run, and I live in Apartment 36 over Goodman's Dry Goods store. He could not understand the realm of my temptation—to steal old McLeod's newspaper or lie to save my son, my son Absalom. He could not understand my fear. It would sound unreal to him who hurls the planets through the skies. How could he sympathize with me, we say of God, as a black man tells a white man, you cannot possibly *feel* for me; you have never been turned down at motel after motel—with your wife sick in the car.

O thou God of love, who reignest in eternity, it is fine to hear about your attributes—and how the theologians have them all categorized—and to know your divine nature; but the mercy I need is mercy in *human* loneliness, and the grace I need is in *human* weakness—and *that* you could not understand. So the veil we draw is the veil of our own frail humanity, too lowly, too earthly to present ourselves with confidence before the throne of grace.

But wait a moment, turn again to the text and go back a line or two and hear the setting of our confidence to approach God. "Since then we have a great high priest who has passed through the heavens, Jesus, the Son of God, let us hold fast our confession. For we have not a high priest who is unable to sympathize with our weaknesses, but one who in every respect has been tempted as we are, yet without sinning." *Then* the writer moves on, "Let us then with confidence draw near to the throne of grace."

Our confidence rests not alone in the divinity we meet in the face of Jesus Christ—such overwhelmingly perfect love could simply drive us further from his throne; our confidence rests as well in Christ's *humanity,* in the knowledge that our loneliness and fear and pain and anguish are well-known to him. When we speak with him, it is to him no foreign tongue. "How well I know," he says, "alas, how well, indeed." "Being found in fashion as a man, he humbled himself, and became obedient unto death." We have not a *high* priest, a remote, abstract, inexperienced, theoretical, impractical priest, who is unable to sympathize with our weaknesses, but one who in every respect has been tempted as we are. Kneeling before him in confession and petition, he hears with the compassion of one who remembers the wilderness beyond the Jordan and the sweat like drops of blood in Gethsemane.

The gravest heresy ever to afflict the Christian Church, like the gravest heresy among us, lay not in the denial of the divinity of Christ, but in the denial of his humanity, and that surprises many twentieth-century Christians. The most stubborn obstacle between us and the throne of grace is not the question of God's godliness (we can affirm the great cosmic impersonal God) but the question of God's humanity. And, of course, this is the crux of the Christian faith— how the two came together in Christ Jesus. "The Word became flesh and dwelt among us, full of grace and truth." Thus when we approach his throne, we approach One who does understand, who has been among us, who has been through it all, and knows whereof we speak. "Let us then with confidence draw near to the throne of grace, that we may receive mercy and find grace to help in time of need."

O God, our Father, behold us a people struggling and torn and sometimes fighting and quarreling, forgetting all about thee and not quite daring to trust thee and making any great, new, bold venture to have thee as companion and support. Take us gently or roughly, as it may be, in our need, and lead us patiently into the presence of him in whom we live and move and have our being, where forgiveness, healing, restoration, and direction are to be found. Amen.

7
THE LORD GOD OMNIPOTENT!

> TEXT: "And Jesus came and said to them,
> 'All authority in heaven and on
> earth has been given to me.'"
> Matt. 28:18

An itinerant minister who fills vacant pulpits Sunday by Sunday told a church pulpit committee he would be happy to come to their church any Sunday of the year but one. "Please," he said, "don't ask me for Easter. I never know what to say." Early Christians felt quite otherwise. Indeed, they changed their day of worship from Saturday to Sunday because Sunday was Resurrection Day, and the Resurrection was *all* they had to say. See how it is in the New Testament: a few pages about the Nativity, a few more devoted to the direct sayings of Jesus, another handful recording the miracles and the parables, but almost all the rest given over to the Easter story and to the events and teachings which deal directly with it and flow from it. In the New Testament the Resurrection is no appendage to the faith: it is the faith!

But, alas, the minister who is at a loss to know what to say on Easter stands not alone in our time. Many honest people must confess grave difficulty in believing the Resurrection story and in holding the Resurrection faith. At the outset, then, what do we mean by the Resurrection faith? Just this: that in Christ Jesus the Eternal God of power and love had the last word, overcoming forever evil and death. That after man had done his worst, thought he had finished things up in his neat, simple way with fear and hatred and jealousy and the skill of his little tools, hammer and sword and spike, God acted. The sign of his action was the reappearance of Jesus—not in a resuscitated human body, but unmistakably, clearly, not as a ghost or phantom but as an undeniable reality among those who had known him best. That in brief is the Resurrection story. God had the last word; and today the Resurrection faith is that God *still* has the last word: that God is God, not death nor the devil, and that perfect love is also perfect power.

With all candor and honesty we must admit that we sometimes find the Resurrection faith difficult to hold. Perhaps then we may take some comfort in discovering that the disciples likewise found the story hard to believe, the faith difficult to embrace. As we read the last chapter of Luke's Gospel we find three causes for unbelief on the part of those who had known Jesus best.

I

First, Luke writes of them in the eleventh verse: "But these words seemed to them an idle tale, and they did not believe them." Just as blunt as that! Dr. Moffatt translated "idle tale" as "nonsense." No beating around the bush with them, no fancy rationalization; the Resurrection—nonsense! Do we not feel at home with them! They had a struggle on their hands, too. An idle tale. This Resurrection story, we say, has been made up in order for the book to come out more pleasantly; a chapter tacked on at the end to alter classic tragedy and to cover up the grim truth of God's abdication on Calvary. No one likes a sad ending, but a sad ending it was, and we might as well accept it. So we have emphasized the teachings of Jesus, held him up as moral example and prized the Bible as literature, but have said of the Resurrection faith: it is an idle tale, nonsense.

But wait a moment. If it be nonsense, then we must in all honesty try to make sense out of facts like these: the Church, for example, or Paul, or the New Testament itself, for they do not explain the Resurrection; the Resurrection rather is the only explanation of them. So it is with all that has followed in their wake: *The Divine Comedy* and *Pilgrim's Progress* and a Bach chorale; Francis of Assisi and Abelard and Augustine; Wesley in the collieries of England and John Watson in the Scottish highlands; Judson in Burma and the Massachusetts Bay Colony; Thomas Hooker and Horace Bushnell; public schools and constitutional law, and your grandfather in church before you and you here this morning. None of them explaining the Resurrection, but all making sense only in the light of its truth. All this because some mysterious thing happened after the crucifixion which caused a handful of men to stop shaking with fear and break out in a glorious doxology: "For thine is the kingdom, and the power, and the glory, for ever. Amen." Those men themselves are hard to understand without the Resurrection. They were broken, dispirited, disillusioned men, fleeing in terror, hiding in fear, trying in every way to disassociate themselves from the Galilean teacher in order to save their own skins. Yet suddenly they were transformed, made dramatically intense, powerful personalities. Was this the work of nonsense, of an idle tale? Strange nonsense *that*, turning cowards into martyrs and splitting the spirit as well as the numbering of the centuries.

But we are arguing the case, and that is not the preacher's role. The point here is clear that to dismiss the Resurrection faith, as the disciples did at first, as an idle tale, simply doesn't make sense. That is name calling. There are better ways to dismiss it than that, if dismiss it we must. Idle tales ordinarily do not stand so powerfully or endure so tenaciously; truth destroys them. We may find the Resurrection incredible, but no thoughtful man can dismiss it as an idle tale—nonsense.

II

The disbelief of the disciples moves to a higher level when we reach the thirty-seventh verse where Luke wrote: "But they were startled and frightened." Here is the disbelief of fear; afraid to believe. Does this not strike closer home? If the Resurrection faith is true, then life does make sense, and we are relieved for a moment . . . but, then, afraid. For if it is true, life does make sense but *only on God's terms*—not on ours! It means we cannot escape his judgment—the defeat of everything ugly; the triumph of everything lovely.

In November, 1950, a bus loaded with a college football team crossed the Continental Divide at Monarch Pass in the Colorado Rockies en route to a neighboring college for a Saturday afternoon game. Monarch Pass crosses the Great

Divide at over 11,000 feet, and as the bus started down the Eastern slope the brakes failed. Anyone who has driven that narrow winding mountain road which goes down three or four thousand feet in five or six miles knows that that football team had quite a ride. The driver wrestled with the steering wheel; the coach broke off the gear shift lever trying to shove it into second, and all the while the players followed the signals called by the driver shifting their considerable corporate weight to the right and to the left to help balance the bus as the driver maneuvered it around curve after curve. Miraculously they reached a straightaway at the bottom going well over one hundred miles an hour and seventeen miles later came to a stop. The story in the newspapers of that incredible escape reported that during the wild ride down the mountain the driver felt something whiz past his head. Later one of the young passengers confessed that what the driver felt was a cheap obscene paperback novel which the lad had thrown away. He explained that he didn't want to be caught dead with that book in his hands. Face to face with the mystery of death, that lad felt judgment breathing down his neck—maybe God does have the last word. Often our disbelief in the Resurrection is not so much finding it difficult to believe but finding it personally fearful to face. The disciples were startled and frightened. Its implications judge us personally and as a people!

The Resurrection means, you see, that God is intent on the fulfillment of his purposes, that he is in dead earnest about the establishment of his kingdom, and that what we are set on is sure to fall in rubbish at our feet and at his, if it is not also what he is set on. It means that the Lord God Omnipotent reigneth and that Herod and Pilate and selfish ambition and intrigue and brutality in the first century and in the twentieth are doomed. It means that the little deceits we get by with do not get us by him; it means that God is God and man is man. It proclaims that all our parochial loyalties to party and class and school and nation are doomed if they are not prompted by love for God and neighbor. If the Resurrection faith be true, it proclaims that the final victory is God's, and that it is on God's terms . . . and the implications of that for our design of living where God is on the periphery and we are planted squarely in the middle are enough to frighten us into comfortable disbelief and to support the wishful thinking which persuades to disbelief in God.

"But they were startled and frightened!" Well, they might have been, and so may we. If God was not content to let things rest as they were on Calvary, he will not be content to let ruthless force or self-serving policies or lies—the big one or the little ones—have the last word today either in Asia or in Washington or in the flowered hills of Berkeley. If the Resurrection be true, then God, the God who was in Jesus Christ, is the one "decisive fact about human life" and when left out, left out of education and foreign policy and marriage and the shaping of economic and political instrumentalities and personal ambition, they have no future. No wonder history is forever being rewritten in blood and anguish, for we try to write it without counting on his determination and then have to back up again and again and start all over. Next time we may have to start from scratch.

III

So it was: at first the disciples called it an idle tale, nonsense, and did not believe; but then they saw its implications and were afraid and did not want to believe. Then, in the third encounter, they still could not believe but for the strangest reason. The record in the forty-first verse brings us these words: "And . . . they still disbelieved for *joy*."

That is not an uncommon reaction to exceedingly good news: some rumor comes that the war is over or that the lost is found or an election won or a cherished position secured and we shake our heads: "No, no, it's too good to be true. I must have heard it wrong!" "But it is, it is true," they say, but we still disbelieve for joy. I wonder if this is not pathetically true among many of us today when we hear the Resurrection faith proclaimed, that God has the last word, that he is not mocked! We have not believed it, really—not many of us in this generation—and we have sophisticatedly buttressed our unbelief with all the little arguments we could muster about ancient documents and folk religion and the lack of scientific data, when all the Resurrection asserts is that the God we know in Christ—the God of utter self-giving love—that that God is God, and he and he alone is the final and complete power and that the best we know in all experience, love, is the everlasting victor.

Perhaps it is a bit to our credit that we have thought it too good to be true. We have seen that life is often tragic and brutal and agonizingly painful, and we have steeled ourselves manfully for the worst; then to have God step in among us and say that the worst is not true, eventually and eternally, but that the *best is,* that is almost too good to be true. We disbelieve for joy.

See what it means, young people with your lovely visions and old people with your wistful dreams. It means that love

74

wisely spent, outpoured in work and reflection, in anticipation and work again is not at last wasted, but is caught up by God and endures. See what it means, men of good will struggling in the classrooms and laboratories, the Parliaments and Main Streets of the world, your struggles are not in vain no matter what the governors of nations declare or what death a guided missile or popular opinion can bring. Pilate governed and the guided spikes brought death, but God has the final government of his creation. The road is not without darkness, the path is not without false turns, the answers are not simple, long life and happiness are not promised; but do not crack under the pressure; do not give in under the strain, for all creation is God's, and God is good and God is all-powerful.

Christ the Lord is risen today. The Lord God omnipotent reigneth! Amen.

8
FIRST THINGS FIRST

TEXT: "Work out the salvation that God
has given you with a proper sense
of awe and responsibility. For it is
God who is at work within you,
giving you the will and the power
to achieve his purpose." Phil. 2: 12-
13 (Phillips)

Imagine if you will a San Francisco cable
car stalled at the level intersection just above the St. Francis
Hotel. The gripman has disappeared, and there doesn't seem
to be anyone around who understands how to get the car
going again. Most of the passengers are not too much concerned, especially the ones who have seats. They are staying
in them and chatting with their neighbors and watching the
traffic moving on up the hill. A few have left the car altogether and have started walking, but they are growing tired
as the hill lengthens ahead of them and have decided to get
aboard if the car catches up with them. The rest are dis-
cussing their dilemma and trying to figure out how to get

the car under way. They hear the cable moving under the surface and out of sight and have the vague suspicion that somehow the car has to get its power from the cable, but no one knows quite how that is done. A few decide that the cable can't be trusted anyway and try to push the car by hand, but it is far too heavy and they only wear themselves out. Almost everyone realizes there is power around somewhere to get them in motion, and they decide to appoint a committee to investigate the problem and make a report, when suddenly the earth begins to tremble ever so slightly but unmistakably and persistently. A terrible sense of urgency begins to pervade their dilemma. They must get going soon or it will be too late.

If we can resist the temptation to push this analogy too far, can we not legitimately see much of our dilemma as modern Protestants in that stalled cable car. We could amuse ourselves greatly by matching all the details, suggesting who it is who has got the comfortable seats and who is chatting and who has decided to get off altogether and who is trying to push it by hand and who is chairman of the report committee, but that would only serve to hide the real nature of the dilemma which is the problem of being separated from the source of power.

It could be cogently argued that in comparison with other periods of our history Protestants are stalled, sitting in their antiquated cable car motionless. Their churches appear to a sympathetic critic as "ghostly reminders of what was once a great religion"—but the earth is trembling, our era is taking on the aspect of New Testament times with serious apocalyptic tones of warning and doom. Is there beneath the surface of this stalled faith a source of power like a moving cable which can again be grasped and relied upon? Is there within the spirit of Protestantism a power to save individuals and preserve us a people of God?

I

Paul Tillich reminds us of one of Albrecht Dürer's engravings which has been called a classic expression of the Protestant spirit. It is entitled "Knight, Death, and the Devil." A knight in full armor is riding through a dark valley. He is accompanied on one side by the figure of death, that haunting mysterious certainty of which we seldom speak, that inevitable fact of human existence which we are considered dreary or morbid to mention. Death on one side of the Knight and on the other a figure of the Devil, that tenacious inclination within us and that unflagging prompting from without us to seek our own, to push in where we don't belong, to brag and rush and hurt and kill: a thorn in the flesh and a perversity of the spirit from Adam in the garden to us in the parking lot. So Death threatening the Knight from one side and the Devil threatening him from the other—but he rides on, confident, erect, eyes ahead, and neither Death nor the Devil confounds him or arrests him. "In his solitude," writes Tillich, "he participates in the power which gives him the courage to affirm himself in spite of the presence" and threatening power of Death and the Devil.[1] If this Knight in truth typifies the Protestant spirit, what sensitive man is there among us who would not like to move clear-eyed and straight ahead to fulfill his destiny as a son of the living God, to lay

[1] *Courage to Be* (New Haven: Yale University Press, 1952), p. 161.

78

hold of the will and the power to achieve God's purpose for him?

It is too casual a reading of history to believe that the Protestant Reformers were heard and followed in the sixteenth century simply because the people were distressed by the conduct of Rome or because the Reformers' teaching aided the ambitions of the German princes. Doubtless both are true, but as that century dawned there was also a profound restlessness in the people: they knew anxiety like our own about Death and the Devil. Otherwise, why do you suppose people of that century could have been bullied into paying large sums to Rome, sums which impoverished them? Why do you suppose they submitted to all sorts of humiliating penance and believed all manner of spiritual nonsense? In no small measure for the same reason that Americans in the twentieth-century rush to buy more and more things while trying to save more and more money and object to social security on political grounds but accept it on practical grounds and religiously obey superficial advice about relieving tensions and follow the cults that promise peace of mind. Like men of our era those sixteenth-century men were ridden with anxiety, afraid to live and afraid to die. Like us, they were frantically trying to work out their own salvation, their own security; they were consumed with fear, and they reached out to anyone who promised a saving word. They were running a losing race with Death and the Devil, as we are running a losing race in this century of science too powerful for our character to manage, a century of guided missiles and unguided ethics, and Martin Luther was running as fast as the best and losing as painfully as the worst.

The spiritual greatness of the Reformers lay in the simple

but astonishing fact that they stopped their running in mid-flight. They turned and faced squarely the depth of their despair, confessed their deep-seated uneasiness, admitted that all their good works and all their costly penance did not ease the dark dread of their souls. Only God could do that. If only God were with them. If only God—not in much busy-ness, not in easy panaceas about relaxing and saying that Death and the Devil are illusions of mortal minds, not in for-getting or adjusting or rationalizing—only in God. But God is holy, perfect, true—and we are profane and imperfect and crude. God is beyond, and we are here. God is without mark or blemish of any sort, and we are spoiled and afraid and weak and unclean and selfish. If only God—but the gulf is great and fixed—and still, still with us death and the devil ride on to harass and to annoy. If only God. . . .

II

Then with flight arrested and with desperate urgency the Reformers turned to the New Testament, and for them, and because of them for us, a new world was opened again, a new source of courage to meet death and the devil was found: the power of the faith that turned the ancient world upside down was laid hold of again, and the Church was refreshed for a new day and was on the move again. They opened the New Testament and found there not systems of penance and mechanical means of grace but a Prodigal Son, in no way worthy of his Father's name or home, and the Father, nonetheless, running out to embrace him while he was still afar off. There they saw that miserable lost sheep and the Shepherd out in the darkness searching for him and hoisting him onto his shoulder rejoicingly; there they found the housewife turning everything topsy-turvy to find one single lost penny. There in the Holy Book—long closed—was the inexhaustible love of God for his Creation written large on every page. And the hallmark of that love was the Cross, with God there making common cause with men, a man without sin dying for wicked men. There was God "so loving the world" and through that love giving men the will and the power to achieve his purpose in their creation.

Our fathers thus learned afresh the meaning of grace, of God's undeserved kindness toward us. If we are to put first things first—this is it. We love God because he first loved us. Our religion is a response to that love, not a frantic effort to win it; it is the difference between the strained worried man trying to be righteous and the joyous grateful man whose righteousness is a spontaneous response to God's graciousness. Death and the devil no longer inspire fear, for God himself is at our side, giving us the will and the power.

When at the close of the service the minister says, "Now may the grace of our Lord Jesus Christ be with you," he is reminding us of this central New Testament and Protestant affirmation. "Our faith," said Luther, "is a lively reckless confidence in the Grace of God."

III

Yet, surely another word must be said. So far that stalled cable car is still there. Someone has come along who has read the book of directions and has explained that there is a cable beneath the surface and that it is strong and lively and dependable, but the car doesn't move until that report is trusted, until someone plunges the gripper beneath the surface of the street and links the car to the source of power.

There is a healthy resurgence today in Protestant circles of concern with the Bible and with theology. Exciting experiments in adult education in many parishes reflect that fresh interest, but it must not stop there. It is necessary to read the report, to see the pictures, to study the diagrams; but all that is not going to move the stalled car. The report must be trusted, the picture must inspire confidence, the diagram must help us not only to understand that there is power beneath the surface but to have the daring to lay hold of it. Ah! there's the rub! And there's the risk! But the risk is set in the midst of a promise—to take the risk is to work at our own salvation with a proper sense of awe and responsibility, trusting that it is God, the gracious God we have heard and seen in Jesus Christ, who is at work within us giving us the will and the power to achieve his purpose.

Almighty God, our Father, our words stand cluttered before thee as we seek to describe the depth and beauty of thy love. But give us this boon: that if there is a stirring deep within us, a new sense of trust in thee, help us to know that it is stirred by thee, for our very disquietude may be the loving prompting of thy Holy Spirit. We ask it through Jesus Christ, our Lord. Amen.

9
GENERATION UNTO GENERATION

TEXT: "The book of the genealogy of Jesus
Christ, the son of David, the son of
Abraham." Matt. 1:1

Two events of abiding significance to this
congregation took place in this place of public worship within
the last ten days. Both of these events were important to us
whether or not we were here or knew the individuals directly
concerned. The first was the funeral of a modest and faithful
man. We gathered in common sorrow as we brought before
God the memory of his life among us, and we praised God,
saying, "Lord, thou hast been our dwelling place in all generations." Within a few days we gathered again and infants
were brought before God in this place to receive the water of
baptism, and we praised God again, saying, "Lord, thou hast
been our dwelling place in all generations."
On the surface these two events may appear to be entirely
separate and disconnected. Yet they took place in the same
building, many of the same persons were present on both
occasions, the same scripture was read, the same God was

praised. We do not have to search our hearts very deeply to sense that far from being disconnected, these two events were inextricably bound together. Each one finds its meaning in the other and, standing together, they movingly symbolize the reality of the Church as a living, organic, visible community.

Will you hold in your mind an awareness of that community, the parish church which we know and in which we participate, as we go back now and pick up this text which on the surface appears about as unpromising as any text we might put forth: "The book of the genealogy of Jesus Christ, the son of David, the son of Abraham." This single verse and the seventeen verses which follow, tracing the generations of Israel, are not tedious archaic genealogy which we can ignore. Rather they celebrate the truth that our faith is rooted in community, that the Bible is not the history of an idea but the history of a people, and that the event of Jesus Christ in the manger of Bethlehem or in our own personal experience cannot be separated from the community in which it takes place. This genealogy with which the New Testament begins presents several important clues to our understanding of the family of God, of the church where we baptize our children, marry our youth, and bury our dead; the particular church on the corner where we pray and quarrel, worship and bicker, and are inspired and depressed.

I

The first clue comes in the simple fact that this text comes first in the New Testament. This dry old genealogy precedes everything else! When Matthew sets about the task of telling the life story of Jesus of Nazareth, he begins not with the story of the birth but with a statement about the community in which that birth took place. The community was the essential setting of the birth; the community did not somehow gather itself around the birth, the birth took place in that setting. The setting was first. Thus the very location of these words—right at the very beginning of the New Testament—underlines the truth of the priority of the Church. Our faith arises from the Church, not the Church from our faith.

Yet we Protestants are forever trying to reverse this order. We entertain the man-centered idea that people somehow hear about Jesus and are attracted to him and decide on their own accord to join in an association of like-minded persons and create the Church. Lesslie Newbigin reminds us rightly "that what our Lord left behind Him was not a book, nor a creed, nor a system of thought, nor a rule of life, but a visible community. . . . The actual community is primary; the understanding of what it is [indeed, the understanding of Him who called it into being] comes second." [1]

We Americans are such experts at organization that it is hard for us to understand this truth about the primary place of the Church, the community of faith. There are many serious-minded folk who have high regard for Jesus Christ. They revere him as a great ethical teacher or they may even honor him as the incarnate God, but frequently they have only disdain for the Church. They do not really face the facts of their own encounter with Christ; they do not honestly consider that without the Church, the continuing community of the new Israel, they would never have met Jesus Christ

---

[1] *The Household of God* (New York: Friendship Press, 1954), pp. 21-22.

himself. They may contend that it is the New Testament which introduced them to their Lord, but the New Testament did not create the Church, the Church created the New Testament. It is not the constitution and by-laws of the early Church, but a report on its meetings and an account of its thought.

Our difficulty in understanding the priority of the Church in Christian experience may arise in part from our unwillingness to confess our dependence upon those who have gone before. Often our haughty contempt for genealogies is an effort to convince ourselves that we are what we are solely by virtue of our own impressive skills. But does a child call his own parents into being or determine when he is sixteen that a family is, after all, a pretty good idea, a convenient way to organize life, and decides forthwith to join one? No, he springs from the family. In truth, he could have no existence apart from the family. If he comes one day to honor its values and to accept them as his own, well and good; but he did not create it. His family is not only a gift to him but the indispensable condition of his existence. Whenever I hear someone declaring his appreciation of Jesus Christ but claiming he will have no truck with the Church because it is so feeble or so corrupt, I think of an old and indelicate saying: It is a foul bird who besmears his own nest.

However, the most loyal churchman must admit that there is grievous truth in the complaint of high-minded persons about the record of the Church. It is not a pretty thing in history with its holy wars and bloody inquisitions, with its built-in resistance in many generations to the claims of love and justice. Nor is its record unblemished in contemporary history, in New Orleans or Berkeley—retreating all too often under the pressure of hysteria and turning pale before yellow journalism. Seeing the dark truth in such charges, many of us want to dissociate ourselves from it. Honor and worship Jesus Christ and labor for him, yes, but confess membership in the Church, no!

II

It is at this point that our text may underline a second fact about the Church: that it is not an association of good men but includes all kinds and conditions of men. Look at this genealogy of Jesus Christ, this naming of the people who were members of the community of God out of which he sprang and of which the Church is the new manifestation. It does not read like a roster of the saints. There are Rahab and Bathsheba, for example, and David himself demonstrating both the nobility and depravity of human nature. If the chief characteristic of the people of God is their moral excellence, then this genealogy needs some serious revision, as, indeed, do the rolls of every local parish I ever heard about. And if the claim of any congregation to be the Church rests in the perfection of its individual members, or in the strength and purity of its witness in society, then the visible Church of God will disappear from the face of the earth. Indeed, with the Church as with the family, when it makes excellence of conduct the condition of membership, it denies the love which creates and sustains it.

Is there then no requirement of membership in the Church? Does the Church just willy-nilly include everyone, a sort of "liberty hall" as Alec Vidler puts it, "where everyone is welcomed and no questions asked." [2] Well, everyone is wel-

[2] *Christian Belief* (London: SCM Press, 1950) p. 84.

comed, but questions *are* asked; however they are not questions of a man's behavior but of his allegiance. Abraham and Bathsheba did not share substantially equal moral achievements—hardly! But they did share a substantially equal acknowledgment of one God above all gods. A man rules himself outside a family not when he fails to live up to his father's love nor even when he deliberately, yea, maliciously disobeys it, but only when he persists in his denial of that love so unrepentantly that for *him,* his father ceases to exist. Perhaps that is the unforgivable sin, the sin against the Holy Spirit, the sin against the Spirit of the Father, so separating ourselves from God that *for us* it really is as though God were not. This is not to claim that the Church is comprehensively inclusive; it is rigorously exclusive, but those who are excluded exclude themselves not by moral failure, though that may be a consequence of it, or by bad tempers, though that may mark God's continued prodding, or by any gross sin, though God hates sin, but by denial of the sovereign love of God revealed in Christ who is the head of the Church.

III

There is a third and final truth about the Church which this ancient text suggests: that *community* does not smother individuals but fosters their fullest life. If we were to read this genealogy in Matthew all the way through, we would end with a sense of the corporate community which was Israel from Abraham to Joseph. And thus far in this sermon we have been emphasizing the corporate nature of the Church. Yet reading that genealogy we could not help being aware also of individuals: Ruth and Uriah and Uzziah; Ahaz, Hezekiah and Amos—individuals, all! What then about the individual in the Church? Is he just lost in the list? Is the Church just one more place where the individual is simply a replaceable unit, a cog in some vast ecclesiastical machinery?

This question demands another sermon: sufficient now to say that every single person who feels that in the Church he is simply a replaceable unit, a cog in the machinery, marks the failure of the Church afresh. If he feels that way, then the Church is not community; it is organization. It is not a divine fellowship but a human institution! It is the failure of the Church at this point which rests most heavily on the heart of every sensitive pastor and every devout layman, and it may be the most serious problem which every large church faces, and one which we hope to face honestly and creatively in planning the future of our parish.

Social diagnosticians are constantly reminding us that we are living increasingly in a society where the old ties which bound men and women to a social group, to family or town or neighborhood, are being dissolved. The average length of residence in a nearby suburb has been disclosed to be three and one-half years, and there are over twenty thousand human beings on the campus adjacent to this church who feel they will be lucky to be *allowed* to stay four years! This mobility, this breaking of old ties, seems at first blush to promise a new order of individual freedom, but a long look at our urban centers full of people who have no ties, where no one knows if they come or go, live or die—replaceable cogs—reveals that this kind of freedom provides its own desolate prison. I was free one Christmas Eve, free and alone in a great city, free to do exactly as I pleased, but never was I more bound and never have I realized more dramatically how impoverished an individual is separated from a community.

We are learning very painfully that far from being restrictive and oppressive, a sense of belonging, a sense of community, is indispensable to the individual. He can only blossom into the full stature of being a man in a community of men, serving and being served, responsible and responsive. To be a human being is to exist with other human beings. In a society which uproots men and throws them into great impersonal centers, clusters will inevitably form; community of a sort may well take place, but will it be community which uses a man as a means or sees him as an end in himself as Christ does?

At a recent meeting of one of the colonies of our parish a young woman told us briefly of her experience growing up in the family of an army officer who was moved every two or three years. "But every place we went," she said, "I found a church and they all seemed much the same. Now, looking back, I realize it was the church, the church in many places, that provided me with a sense of belonging, of having a home." I dare say that girl took some initiative herself in getting acquainted, but nonetheless the church provided a community in which she was sustained and supported through critical years.

Yet do you sense how easy it would be for me now to conclude this sermon as one of your pastors with an earnest exhortation for everyone to get up and glad hand the person next to him and cultivate a sort of cheeriness—a smile which lasts to the parking lot? American Protestantism is already mired in this soupy trap trying to solve the deep human need for fellowship by superimposing it on the parish church like a sweet icing on a cake. We have multiplied our clubs and societies and coffee hours as though in themselves they could meet this problem, and their success rests on the presupposition that everyone in the Church is good and therefore will be congenial with everyone else. Well, everyone in the Church is not good, nor does God demand it as a condition of membership; and everyone in the Church cannot possibly like everyone else; they don't even all like the ministers. Alas, it would be a frail fellowship we would possess on the basis of mutual attractiveness, on the premise of everyone being happy about everything. It would take a spineless pulpit and a sleeping pew to produce that kind of fellowship, and it would possess about as much community as a cemetery, marked only by proximity of location.

The community which will save us, which will enable us to love one another even when we don't always like one another, which will provide us with the charity to make this parish a place where everyone, black or white, Republican or Democrat, eighteen or eighty, the inner motivated and outer motivated, the town and the gown, the shy and the brash, *everyone* feel at home, will be the community of faith, the community which is bound not superficially and temporarily, but profoundly and through all eternity, by a common allegiance to the one God we have met in the face of Jesus Christ. It will be the community where our clubs and our societies and our coffee hours, as well as our funerals and our baptisms, declare with one voice before God and man, "Lord, thou hast been our dwelling place in all generations."

Almighty God, the God and Father of our Lord Jesus Christ, of thine infinite mercy thou hast called us into thy Church; grant us thy favor and establish thou the work of our hands in our time and in our place, for Jesus' sake. Amen.

10
PERILS OF PRIVATE PIETY

TEXT: ". . . that you . . . may be able to grasp (with all Christians) how wide and deep and long and high is the love of Christ—. . . ." Eph. 3:18 (Phillips)

A returning student greeted me warmly a few days ago and reported a busy summer and then added, as though he thought I should be warned, "I'm afraid you won't be seeing me around the church much this year now that I've taken on an outside job, but then I guess I can say my prayers just as well by myself." I agreed with him at once, partly because I didn't want him to think for one minute that I was stuffy about church attendance. Ministers have to appear very casual about matters like that or else they will scare everybody away, especially students and other busy people, with the thought that Christian faith *requires* anything. If this chap had stood still a little longer I would have reminded him—in order to make him understand how accepting I really am—that Jesus taught us to go into the closet and close the door when we pray; or if that failed to reassure him, I would have quoted the famous philosopher who said "religion is what a man does with his solitariness." If you can believe the record, both Jesus and the famous philosopher seem to support this student's contention that he can say his prayers just as well by himself. In saying that, he was making a declaration of independence from the church, announcing that his piety, his prayers, his religious exercises and practices this year anyway were going to be a private affair, one man alone with God.

Now in a very profound sense all true piety *is* private! There is, I presume, nothing else in life so intensely private, personal, inward, resolutely exclusive as a person's religion. There are experiences in this area which by their very nature cannot be shared, sighs too deep for words. The tear-stained, penitential, forgiving, open-armed reunion of the Prodigal and his father is not a public convention but is an extravagantly private, personal affair, soul meeting soul! Religious experience, practice, and piety—all have their irrevocably private aspects.

Surely Paul was remembering his own tremendously personal experience when he wrote to the Ephesians hoping that they would be able to comprehend, be able to grasp, how wide and deep and long and high is the love of Christ! Yet, I wonder if Paul was not thinking of some of the perils of private piety when he inserted, parenthetically, in this very sentence, those three telling words, "with all Christians." "I pray . . . that you . . . may be able to grasp (with all Christians)" or in the older translations, "comprehend with all saints" or "with all God's people how wide and deep and long and high is the love of Christ." The full measure, the

94

breadth and length and depth and height of the love of Christ, the full expanse of the Christian life can never be experienced alone. This is not a matter of *either/or* but *both/and!* We can easily see how impoverished and stunted a thing is the religion of the vigorously active churchman who avoids at all costs private piety, the personal searching encounter, the deep, deep questions. It is not uncommon for the ministers of this parish to suggest to such a person that he slow down in parish involvement and give God a chance for a personal encounter! This morning, however, look at the other side: private piety becomes a stunted and impoverished thing without the public corporate experience in the community of faith. "I pray . . . that you . . . may be able to grasp (with all Christians) . . . the love of Christ." That is a condition of grasping the fullness of that love for many reasons. Consider two of them.

I

Private piety is not enough, in the first place, because every Christian needs the corporate *memory* of the Church: the scriptures, the sacraments, the worship, the tradition—this is the invaluable stored-up corporate memory of all Christians in all time which supports and disciplines the private piety of every believer. You recall that well-known story of Philip of Macedon, the father of Alexander the Great, who had a slave to whom he assigned an unusual task. The slave was required to come to his room every morning and coldly interrupt whatever the king was doing or thinking with these words: "Remember, Philip, thou must die." Private piety is thus constantly interrupted by the memory of the Church. That memory may remind us, as Philip's slave did, of our mortality, for this is the unchanging perspective of existence which we often forget or deny or it may keep our vision balanced in any number of considerations. A man praying only in his room may forget what the memory of the Church keeps alive.

Without the memory of the Church we may see our situation as being either much better or much worse than it actually is! The idealistic optimists who arrive at a "cultural lag" theory of human evil see us much better off than we are. The classical cynics who believe the human situation is hopeless see us as much worse off than we are. Both may retire to their rooms to pray, but even their praying is imperiled because neither possesses in himself the memory of the Church which would, for the one, discipline his faulty optimism, and for the other, relieve his false despair. Of course, if the Church abandons its own memory by closing its Book or drugging its prophets or neglecting its intellectual history and allowing its educational function to wither, it will not offer this guard against the perils of private piety! Indeed, the impoverished condition of much of American Protestantism may lie in the fact that its memory has been so dimmed by its cultural and intellectual accommodations that it has become senile, deserving only to be treated courteously but not to be taken seriously.

The common memory of the Church also corrects our piety because the Church eventually remembers what we, if left to our own devices, tend to forget. In the private practice of religion we are selective. We hear what we want to hear and remember what is not too painful to remember. For example, my friend who is going to be a Christian on his own hook in splendid isolation this year will undoubtedly select those passages of Scripture for his private prayers that he knows or likes or understands! But the Church remembers not only the twenty-third Psalm and the thirteenth chapter of I Corinthians; it also holds Amos who thunders questions about how a man earns and spends his money and enshrines the searching denunciation of Jesus on religious frauds! Indeed, many a man has retreated into the cave of private piety because he came one day into the community of believers and heard the words of Jesus and sensed the inescapable conclusion that there were very discomforting memories which the community of believers keeps alive—memories to haunt a man who rushes around building barns all the time: barns to store things and grudges and suspicions. The memory of the Church puts the heat on us, if you will, melting us down out of the frozen forms which undisciplined private piety may cake around us as a hiding place for the full life which lies dormant in every man. "I pray . . . that you . . . may be able to grasp (with all Christians) how wide and deep and long and high is the love of Christ."

II

In the second place, private piety is not enough because alone *it tends to aggravate rather than heal our fundamental human sickness which is loneliness,* a haunting frightening sense of standing all alone, of being deeply separated from one another and from that for which we were intended. My young friend who plans to shy clear of the church this year and limit his formal religious practice to praying by himself may be planning to do so, as he says, because he is pressed for time. But I wonder! I really wonder, because as he moves into a more isolated kind of life he is also moving further away

97

from people, and we are not created to live in isolation but to love and be loved and to exist in relationship with people.

In one of his books Reuel Howe writes, "God created *persons* to be loved and *things* to be used . . . however, we are always tempted to love things and use persons." In his proposed isolation this chap is pulling away from persons: separated from them he can still *use* them, *use* their books, their wisdom, their gifts, their medicine, their law, their culture— he can even love *their usefulness,* but separated from them he cannot in truth *love* them. If his private piety becomes a way of life, in twenty years he may be isolated almost wholly from people in the pursuit of things or ideas. But why? We who were created for one another and for God—why do we run from people to things, from relationships to isolation?

The Church seems always to be scolding people who seem to love *things* inordinately, but the Church—the community of believers—may be responsible for that inordinate love for things. It is, if these people have discovered in the Church as they have elsewhere that it pays to love things rather than persons because things cannot hurt you, things cannot reject you, things cannot go off and die and leave you abandoned —more alone than before you knew what love might be— but people can do all this. People can hurt, and running from them to any kind of seclusion or private piety or the pursuit of things or much busyness, even busyness for good causes, further aggravates our human sickness of loneliness.

All of us in some measure at some time are like the little rich boy of tradition and of fact, standing in his proper Eton collar behind his gate day after day looking out at children, the ordinary children, playing in the street. He had magnificent toys, but they had each other. And then one day he took his courage in his hand and opened the gate and went out. But he was different and the others were jealous or frightened or afraid, and to protect themselves and to protect their own tenuous solidarity—and is this not the key to American race problems—they laughed at him. And he ran back inside the gate and wrapped himself in toys and more toys and in a deeper, deeper loneliness. Other persons in their own fearfulness and loneliness enlarge ours, and the dreadful cycle deepens as it narrows. But in this world of persons, this world of persons who can hurt, it is also magnificently and mysteriously true that healing comes only through persons, too, not through things or ideas or self-improvement but through persons.

Several years ago a physician, Dr. Frederic Wertham, in a study of pain published in the *Atlantic Monthly*, reported that while undergoing an operation without anesthetic even the accidental touch of a human hand was enough to penetrate and relieve the terrible isolation and loneliness of his world of pain. It takes persons to get through to persons in hurting and in healing, too. The child hurt by his playmate runs to his mother, to a person, not just any person, but to one with whom he feels safe. In and through that same person healing of the hurt and easing of the loneliness begins. That same person does not in herself possess the power to heal, but in her caring and in her loving and in her listening she is the agent of it for Him from whom all healing comes.

III

Cynics laugh at the words "old mother church," yet the phrase is not without its point, for the Church is that community whatever it may be called, however hidden or partial it may be, where people feel safe and being loved by God *through* other people are able to respond in love to others. In that experience, hurts begin to heal and loneliness begins to ease, and we begin to grasp with all Christians the breadth and depth and length and height of the love of Christ. The personal question for each one of us who calls himself Christian is this: how *safe* are others with us—if they risk approach to the citadel of ourselves, will they find healing or only another hurt?

There is an ancient prayer you may remember entitled "A Prayer for the Right Use of Affliction." It includes these words, "that, when we shall have served Thee in our generation, we may be gathered unto our fathers, having the testimony of a good conscience; [and] in the communion of Thy holy Church . . ." [3] "The communion of Thy holy Church." For people who regard grace as a mechanical matter that phrase may mean that one is safe when he dies if he has met the outward requirements to be considered "in the communion of Thy holy Church." But for those who have experienced the actual grace of God, with their hurts eased and their loneliness brought to an end know that that phrase, "the communion of Thy holy Church," may well mean that relationship with other people where they found their hurts healed, their loneliness ended—not the loneliness of an empty afternoon, but the loneliness of an empty life—for strange as it may be God only comes to persons through persons.

Private piety, religion all locked up in the closet of our own souls, seems like a pretty insipid and selfish thing along-

[3] *Book of Common Worship* (Philadelphia: The Westminster Press, 1933) p. 97.

side the beauty of a religion that encourages us to risk new relationships, because having had our own loneliness ended, we cannot wait to be the instrument to end the loneliness of another. Surely it is God's purpose for us as a parish people to be a people of God, a community where *things* are *used* and people are *loved,* and God is thus glorified and enjoyed forever.

Almighty God, our heavenly father, for all this which we believe to be true and have said among ourselves, we praise thy name. We only know and trust thy love because of that divine person who has come to us, taking upon himself all the pain of our loneliness and all the wounds of our separation. For him and all other persons in whom we have seen thy love we give thee thanks and pray that we ourselves may become gentle instruments of thy healing and of thy reconciliation. We ask it in his name whom we call Lord and own as master. Amen.

11

BUILT INTO A SPIRITUAL HOUSE

TEXT: "Like living stones be yourselves built into a spiritual house, to be a holy priesthood." I Pet. 2:5

Some of the basic affirmations of Protestantism sound abstract, theoretical, and their implications are hazy and remote, but the one before us today bears with a practical sort of clarity and immediacy because it deals with the place of every believer in the Church. In pre-Reformation times the clergy had come to rule the Church and were a class of persons set aside—the spiritual elite—with special power and privilege denied the ordinary layman. Martin Luther struck out at this theory and practice when he attacked the concept of ordination as a sacrament. Making ordination a sacrament, he wrote,

was designed to engender implacable discord whereby the clergy and the laity should be separated farther than heaven and earth, ... This is the source of that detestable tyranny over the laity by the clergy who, . . . not only exalt themselves above lay Christians, . . . but even regard them [laymen] as dogs, unworthy to be included with them in the Church. . . . Here Christian

102

brotherhood has expired and shepherds have become wolves. All of us who have been baptized are priests without distinction.[1]

Thus, a basic doctrine of Protestantism began to be formulated, and another New Testament truth and practice was revived which we call "the priesthood of all believers." The charge was leveled against Luther that he thus took all the priests out of the high and holy place of the sanctuary and reduced them all to the common estate of the pew. Not so, the Reformers replied, quite to the contrary; our faith takes all the so-called common men out of the pews and elevates them to the high dignity and responsibility of the true priesthood.

For many Protestants today the doctrine of the priesthood of all believers has come to mean only that every believer has direct access to the throne of God, that faith and repentance are the only requirements for forgiveness and that the believer needs no priest to be his intercessor. However, the doctrine of the priesthood of all believers is twisted and perverted when it is used to support a highly individualistic view of Christian experience. A main thrust of this doctrine is to underline the religious responsibility which every Christian believer bears for his neighbor. The priest, even in Luther's day, was not an isolated monk working out his own salvation in lonely splendor, but a man who was an agent, a channel, an intercessor for other men. When Protestants affirm the priesthood of all believers, they are saying that this responsibility is not one that we can put off on someone else, some hired ecclesiastical hand, but that every believer is required

[1] Roland Bainton, *Here I Stand* (Nashville: Abingdon Press, 1950), p. 138.

by God to be a priest to his neighbor. Protestants who celebrate the Lord's Supper seated in the pews, dramatically symbolize the priesthood of all believers, for here at the Lord's Table we are actually served the elements by our neighbor in the pew and in turn serve our neighbor.

This doctrine places as heavy a religious responsibility upon every believer as it does upon the clergy. It disavows a caste system in the Church. The congregation appoints some to serve as ministers, some as deacons, some as teachers, but they all have a priesthood to exercise. Once when ordaining some young men to preach, Luther in his forthright manner admonished them, "Begone, young men, and do not enter upon this holy estate unless you are . . . able to believe that you are not made one whit better than the laity."

This is a heady doctrine which does not sit easily in modern Protestantism, despite the healthy determination of many laymen that the preacher is not to run the church. Although we give lip service to the idea of the priesthood of all believers, many of us simply do not want to be *that* Protestant. We need a devout and wise and eloquent ministry, to be sure, but we have continued to set the minister apart and demanded of him a spirituality and religious gifts and ethical behavior which we have not been willing to demand of ourselves. We have offered him special privileges like discounts and exemption from parking tickets which the clergy have been all too willing to accept; but have, in turn, demanded special behavior. We have looked askance at him if he drove a convertible and could not understand how his children could be little monsters like our own. Our age of specialization has reached its confining arm into the Church and put the ministers into the role of specialists in Christianity and allowed religion for the layman to become another one of the spectator activities. The new reformation of the Church, its renewal and refreshment in our time, may well come as Protestants take seriously the holy priesthood to which every believer is called.

However, the laymen of the Church may well resent any suggestion that they have not assumed their responsibilities as churchmen. With all due respect to the ministers of this church, both past and present, it must be confessed that here, as in every vital Protestant church, the continuous strength of the parish year in and year out does not lie primarily with the ministers. The miracle is that some of our churches survive some of their ministers. The continuing strength is in the laity. That is dramatically true in this parish. In last Sunday's calendar there was printed a list of about eighty names of members of this parish who seldom worship with us on Sunday morning because they are being priests and carrying the quiet but taxing responsibility of our excellent church school. See this choir overflowing the choir loft—100 per cent volunteer—giving hours every month to assist us in the worship of God. In the enthusiastically supported seminar program this fall, the leadership is almost exclusively composed of members of this parish. It would be impossible to name the hundreds of people who spend hours a week continuing the work of this one parish in Berkeley and around the world. In our radio congregation are scores of people confined to their rooms who would gladly tell of the ministry of this church to them largely through ordinary members of the parish.

Yet, honesty compels us to confess that increasingly Protes-

tants have turned the spiritual side of the church work over
to the clergy. Laymen respond very willingly to requests to
tend to the functioning of the church as a business organization—and thank the powers that be that they do—but, my
word, think of the consternation that would be caused if at
the end of this sermon I invited Brother So-and-So to lead us
in prayer. "Why," someone would whisper to his neighbor,
"I don't think he's even *ordained!*" Such an incident would
undoubtedly unnerve us, at least it would unnerve the one
elected to pray; but there have been times, times when
Protestantism was strong, when such a request would have
seemed quite natural and legitimate.

I am not proposing so to violate what we call the dignity
of our services, but I am suggesting that one of the minister's chief responsibilities is to assist every believer in the
exercise of his own priesthood. The clergy who take upon
themselves all the religious functions of the church and per-
petuate the ideas of two classes of Christians, professional and
amateur, full time or part time, are mostly to blame for the
weakness of the life and witness of the church in our time;
and laymen who consent to that division conspire in a repu-
diation of the peculiar strength of Protestantism. However, a
harangue is out of place; better to suggest some practical
measures we may take together to restore to effectiveness
among us the doctrine of the priesthood of all believers.

I

In the first place, to be effective priests, laymen as well as
clergymen need to be able to give an account of the faith
they hold. It is a very rare thing for a layman to take excep-

106

tion to something the minister says on the basis of his own reading and understanding of the Bible or in terms of his own Christian experience. Many laymen are simply lost in a vague hazy and often sentimental religious fog. The church which expects its laymen to stand up and be counted in their vocations and in their community on ethical and moral issues when it has not provided opportunities for those laymen to study together even the teachings of Jesus is certainly expecting too much. And laymen who pontificate on "the Christian way of life" but who never open their Bibles make public the private shame of the church. Go home and write out a personal credo—This I believe. Put it away and then for a year be faithful in public worship and private prayer and study and then read it over again. If it has changed and grown and deepened—if it is clearer and stronger and seems nearer the mind of Christ—then we will have made progress in reestablishing the priesthood of all believers.

II

In the second place, to be effective priests we need to develop Christian imagination about our neighbor. We need to try to put ourselves in his shoes and enfold him not only with our mind but with our imagination. The good priest bears his neighbor's burden, and tries to lighten his load. Few Christian congregations today reject the obviously poor, the obviously unbalanced, the obviously unattractive; or, at least, they have an uneasy conscience if they do. They have heard too much about deacons foreclosing mortgages on widows' houses to want to provide a character study for some contemporary Sinclair Lewis. Christ has got that far into the midst of the sorriest parish church. Those scandals belong to another day. But a new dimension can be added to the priest-hood we exercise to one another if we allow Christ to take command of our imagination and enable us to pick up the burden we cannot understand. When death invades a home in this parish everyone rushes in to help if he can; the sympathizing tear flows readily and brings much comfort. But the grief which death brings is an obvious burden. Only the crude or cruel will not sympathize. But there is a deeper grief, a more pervasive estrangement than the one death brings, a grief whose only outward sign may be a pinched face or a sharp tongue; and what then if our neighbor is edgy or ugly or perverse or stingy or narrow, do we rush in to help with that burden too? When a man acts that way, he is hurt or afraid or embittered or unloved. Can we as priests of Christ offer him in Christ's name the miracle of a fellow-ship born of a love too deep for words? No one would ever guess what is hidden behind the outward facade of our re-spectability on a Sunday morning; Christ asks us to guess and to offer his understanding and his love. The congrega-tion which can sing with the voice of lovely experience,

> We share each other's woes,
> Each other's burdens bear
> And often for each other flows
> The sympathizing tear,

has begun to bring to life again the doctrine of the priesthood of all believers.

III

Finally to be a priest is a full-time occupation exercised all day every day. If we are to be priests in the Protestant fashion, then that priesthood is not fulfilled just when we are at church or at our prayers. Elton Trueblood has suggested that the local parish church should be a launching pad for the Christian, "a place from which people engaged in secular life are propelled. . . . The person who supposes that he can be a Christian by observing a performance, whether of the Mass or anything else, has missed the whole idea." If our priesthood is something we exercise just in the church and among church friends, then we have missed the essence of Protestantism and have not heard the invitation of Jesus, not just to be his disciples in a private little elite religious group, but to be his apostles moving out into the whole world. If the office in which you work or the classroom in which you teach or the dormitory in which you live is no different because you are there, you who have said you believe in Jesus Christ and accept him as your Lord, you who are called to a holy priesthood, if it just doesn't make any difference, then ask your Lord again today to go with you. Indeed, he may come this time to your support through some ordinary Christian, a neighbor here in the community of faith who is taking his own priesthood with new seriousness.

> Blest be the tie that binds
> Our hearts in Christian love:
> The fellowship of kindred minds
> Is like to that above.

O God our Father, whose son our Saviour hast sent us forth to carry the gospel into all the world, abide now with thy people and accompany us in all our going and coming that it may be to the glory of thy holy name. Amen.

12
OUT OF THE DITCH

TEXT: "At that time Jesus went through the grainfields on the sabbath; his disciples were hungry, and they began to pluck ears of grain and to eat. But when Pharisees saw it, they said to him, 'Look, your disciples are doing what is not lawful to do on the sabbath.' He said to them, 'Have you not read what David did, when he was hungry, and those who were with him: how he entered the house of God and ate the bread of the Presence, which it was not lawful for him to eat nor for those who were with him, but only for the priests? Or have you not read in the law how on the sabbath the priests in the temple profane the sabbath, and are guiltless? I tell you, something greater than the temple is here. And if you had known what this means, "I desire mercy, and not sacrifice," you would not have condemned the guiltless. For the Son of man is lord of the sabbath.'

"And he went on from there, and entered their synagogue. And behold, there was a man with a withered hand. And they asked him, 'Is it lawful to heal on the sabbath?' so that they might accuse him. He said to them, 'What man of you, if he has one sheep and it falls into a pit on the sabbath, will not lay hold of it and lift it out? Of how much more value is a man than a sheep! So it is lawful to do good on the sabbath.' Then he said to the man, 'Stretch out your hand.' And the man stretched it out, and it was restored, whole like the other. But the Pharisees went out and took counsel against him, how to destroy him."   Matt. 12:1-14

Did you notice the unexpected and terrifying twist in the very last sentence of that lesson? The verse moves along very nicely reporting a conversation between Jesus and a group of Pharisees. To us in our time the record sounds harmless enough: Jesus points out that people are more important than animals, and then he heals a crippled man and generally affirms the dictum "the better the day the better the deed." And in response to all that the Pharisees are furious. Indeed, they begin the conspiracy against him, becoming his determined enemies. When we examine this text closely we begin to see not only what upset these Pharisees, but the revolutionary scale of values upon which Christians are required by their Lord to make ethical decisions both publicly and privately. See what made these Pharisees so angry.

I

In the first place, they were upset because Jesus unsettled their religious security. The Pharisees were earnest and sincere men, no doubt of that, religious men who believed that the law was the final and absolute and holy will of God and to obey it down to its last final detail was the simplest way to be sure of God's favor and to be secure ultimately. If they had been concerned only to obey the Ten Commandments, that would have been one thing. Or if they had been concerned only to obey the law as it is developed in the first five books of the Bible, that would have been another thing. But what concerned them was the scribal or oral law which attempted to prescribe for every possible circumstance of life. In the case of the sabbath law, it defined hundreds of petty rules and regulations. On the sabbath day no one is to work, as everyone knows; but what is work? To answer that question they developed thirty-nine categories, and in one of them work was described as carrying a burden. But that provoked the further question, what is a burden? So many pages of details were worked out describing the nature of a burden. A burden, for example, is milk enough for a gulp or honey enough to put on a sore or a pebble big enough to throw at a bird. And the Pharisees found their religious security in bending every effort to obey these laws, to be moral men in this limited and absurdly legalistic fashion.

When Jesus gave them this new teaching about the sabbath —"the sabbath was made for man, and not man for the sabbath"—he turned all this upside down immediately, as we can see. He made it clear that it wasn't enough to obey the letter of the law, that you had to make your own judgments, you had to establish your own list of priorities, you had to have a basis for ethical judgments that was warm and living and that rested in quite a different place than the law. He said that there are greater and lesser commandments, and that every decision has to be made in the light of its particular circumstances. Now one would think that the Pharisees would have been delighted to be relieved of the burden of the laws, but they were not. They were upset and angry for the same reason that we would be and sometimes are: their religious security had just been unsettled. Difficult as it might be to live up to the law, still if one knows what it is, there is a certain security in knowing where you stand and in not having to make all these decisions yourself. Individual responsibility is lessened.

We have passed through a period of Protestant religious history when the law almost took over again, and Protestantism was viewed in many quarters as a moralistic religion hedged in and cribbed about and defined by countless laws, big ones and little ones. Many of the young people of our homes who have turned away from Protestant religion in our time have turned away because this is all they ever heard of Protestantism, a religion of behavior and of little laws. Some of us even got caught up in the same problem about sabbath observance that the Pharisees did. I don't know how it was in your home, but in our home when I was a child we had laws like this about the sabbath: we could play rook, but we couldn't play bridge; we could go to a concert, but we couldn't go to a movie. Such laws can become complex and hard to defend, yet many of us are reluctant to see these laws and regulations disregarded because without them we have the responsibility to see what true sabbath observance is and to come to our own decisions about what really constitutes responsible Christian behavior.

We understand the problem of the law versus individual responsibility in other realms and acknowledge the necessity of the law in the light of human responsibility. If a maximum speed law on our highway is replaced by a law, as it has been in some states, that requires only a "safe and reasonable speed," then this new freedom from the law places personal responsibility upon each driver. He can no longer lean on the law and have that mechanical security of knowing he is not going to be stopped, no matter how fast he drives so long as he doesn't go over sixty-five. But if he does not have that law, he must always be questioning himself; is this a safe and reasonable speed under these particular conditions? As a driver, am I an acceptable citizen? So it is in the final religious question: As a person, am I acceptable to God? or in the old biblical phrase, what must I do to be saved? Is the answer to that question a mechanical one? Just repeat some formula, "I believe in Jesus Christ," or go through some ritual, be baptized or join the church, or obey some rigid standards—never swearing or stealing or lying? Then what a comfortable thing the law is, and how secure we are! But if the answer to that question is not a mechanical answer, but is warm and deep and broad and living and says something about casting one's entire dependence upon God, of depending upon him and seeking to know his will as it develops and unfolds day by day and enter into a living relationship with one's Creator, then we must always remain alert and on tiptoe and can never be sure, never be certain, always bear the responsibility to be responsible, that is "responsive" to perfect love, to God disclosed in Christ.

Some weeks ago an angry woman called me anonymously on the telephone and engaged in a long and heated tirade against her neighbor who had broken, she said, one of the Ten Commandments—the worst one. She was very smug, she was safe and very self-righteous and, as she made perfectly clear, *she* had *not* broken that Commandment. And yet if she, by chance, were to hear again the words of Jesus overarching the law about adultery with the law or word of love for neighbor, self-giving, patient long-suffering love, what might her response then be? Would not that religious security which rests in the knowledge of what laws one has not broken be seriously shaken? When we begin to understand that being a Christian is not secured simply by obeying the law and by being good people who attend church regularly and read the Bible for ten minutes a day, when we begin to sense that the Christian life is not secured even by believing all the right doctrines that come fresh from the theological seminaries—but that it is a total responsible relationship to God, a manner or fashion of our whole existence which may cancel the law, then we see that a frightening new responsibility accompanies the new freedom. Then these easier guarantees and securities in law and creed and dogma and church recede into their proper and useful places. They are supports for our weakness, means made necessary by our frailty but not guarantees or ends. The Pharisees did not like to have their religious security unsettled nor do we, yet we must be thoroughly shaken of these partial and inadequate securities to be prepared to understand that faith in the Christian sense is not doctrinal or moralistic, primarily, but a matter of a whole new point of view—a relationship to God and neighbor and the whole creation.

II

In the second place, the Pharisees were angered not only because Jesus upset their religious security but because he put such a high value on persons—on all persons. Jesus asked them, "What man of you, if he has one sheep and it falls into the ditch on the sabbath, will not lay hold of it and lift it out?" It is presumed that the Pharisees answered, "Of course, any man would do that," for they knew that it was lawful to do so, that every man was entitled to protect his own property. Then Jesus went on, "Of how much more value is a man than a sheep!" Through the years it has been suggested that the Pharisees may have replied to that question: "Well, sir, that depends on the price of wool." Indeed, they may have so answered! At least some men in every generation to our own have put property ahead of persons. The great moral revolution made by Christianity is nowhere clearer than in this question about human rights where a man is declared to be more important than the sabbath, and a person declared to be more important than a sheep or any other property. The

great social issues have almost always centered on this con-
flict—property or persons, a sheep or a man. Prison reform,
child labor, narcotics control, gambling, slavery, war—in
every such issue in Western society there has always come a
striving for improvement when honest, sensitive men who
have truly sought to love the God revealed in Jesus Christ
have been faced with the shaking, practical implications of
the fact that this quotation from Scripture is not a question
Jesus asks but a declaration he makes: "Of how much more
value is a man than a sheep!" He is not asking us, he is telling
us!

Well, of how much more value is a man than a sheep—or
a house? Well, that depends on the color of the man and the
location of the house. Not so, says Jesus. A house is of passing value, but a man is of eternal value. Of how much more
value is a man than a luxury meal? Well, that depends on
whether that man lives in Berkeley or Hong Kong. Not so,
says Jesus. Luxury is of passing value, a man is of eternal
value. Of how much more value is a man than a political
system or a theological system or a penal theory? Ah—not
so, not so. Do you see why the Pharisees were angry with
Jesus? I feel some of this same anger myself. For he puts us
on the defensive, he threatens us, he shows us up. I have not
wanted to preach from this text because this single, unquali-
fied teaching of our Lord is absolutely clear, and we cannot
walk around it. You may argue about its implications and
how it should be applied, but there is no getting around the
truth of it. Christian ethics is not based on some abstract,
general, theological or theoretical idea of the Absolute Good,
but it regards man who is God's creature and child as the supreme good. When Jesus is quizzed about ethics he does not

come up with a theory, he comes up with people—people everywhere: a man beaten by robbers and left half dead on a dusty road; a boy off in a far country, Los Angeles, Chicago, or Paris wasting his life with whores; some hungry men in a grainfield on a sabbath day; a man with a withered hand praying in church, and some foreign student or decorated veteran or ordinary American citizen who finds no room in a half-empty inn. We may disagree about what Christians should do with these problems but to be indifferent to them or to deny them is to be faithless to our Lord.

III

This brings us to the third and most embarrassing reason why the Pharisees were upset by Jesus' teaching about the sabbath, and I suspect it is the reason that upsets us most, too; at least, it does me. It is just this: *Jesus didn't just philosophize or theorize or dream about people and how important they were or only talk about people who were far away and could be safely loved by remote control or by proxy through some missionary or gift or Peace Corps. But he demonstrated at once that by people he meant the people right close at hand.* See how the text moves along. The Pharisees point to the man with the withered hand. To them he is an object lesson, an illustration. He only provokes a question for them to ask. Jesus answers their question, but he immediately turns to the man right there and pours out his healing concern for him. The Pharisees kept people at a distance; Jesus moved right in. This angered them, and it certainly troubles me. For we are very skillful at keeping a safe distance from people and then try to love them at arm's length.

For one thing, we keep them at arm's length by keeping

them in groups. Now that's a good way. Some older people in this parish complain to me about our thoughtless younger generation, and then I ask them, "But do you mean so and so?" and usually name one of their friend's grandchildren. And then they say, "Oh, no, of course not; I *know* him." And then some of the young people come and complain about some of the old people who are fuddyduddies and who don't understand modern youth, and I ask, "Do you mean Mr. Blank or Miss So and So?" and then they look at me with disgust. "Why, of course not," they say, "we *know* him or her." Old people, young people, racial groups, professional groups, whenever we keep thinking of people in the mass, in groups, we protect ourselves against the painful personal encounter which is absolutely essential to Christian love.

Or we keep people at arm's length or further by labeling them. We type them, categorize them, and then file them away like an old answered letter. What a wonderful surprise it is when we discover that we have made a bad mistake and someone we have filed away under the category of unreasonable or impossible or difficult or touchy turns out to be reasonable and quite possible, not difficult or touchy at all if *we* have had a good night's sleep!

Or we pity people instead of loving them, and that is another way to hold them at arm's length. Pity is part of love, to be sure, and in it we share the desolation and separation of people, but love is larger and more comprehensive. Pity is condescending, but love comes down under the loss of another man and shares it and enters into it.

There is another very clever way some of us have of keeping people at a safe distance so we really never love them, and that is by not thinking of the people nearest to us as people at all. Some of us live with people we do not know, and we work with people we do not even see, and yet often the people most starved for consideration as persons are not the oppressed and distant masses teeming on foreign shores but the people we work with every day and know in our own homes. Many an idealistic youth ready to go to Africa to bind up the wounds of the afflicted knocks his own parents into the ditch in his heedless rush out the front door. Some of the most tragic little chapters in history deal with the forgotten families of men who were out busy reforming society. One of the saddest things of all is to keep our own loved ones at arm's length and not really know them.

Do you remember that unburdening conversation in the novel, *The Edge of Sadness,* between two priests who had been childhood chums. The bitterness which one of them finally expresses touches fearful depths but is couched in the recollection of his father's skillful belittling of his mother over a meal. A roast chicken, delicately rejected, is the instrument of a cruelty deeper, perhaps, than drunkenness or adultery or failure to provide. He plagued her and humiliated her without any great offense as the world views offense. To keep our own loved ones at arm's length is to bemean and to deny the appellation "loved one."

The basis for all our decisions comes in other words, too. "Love is patient; love is kind and envies no one. Love is never boastful, nor conceited, nor rude; never selfish, not quick to take offence. Love keeps no score of wrongs; does not gloat over other men's sins, but delights in the truth. There is nothing love cannot face; there is no limit to its faith, its hope, and its endurance.

"In a word, there are three things that last for ever: faith, hope, and love; but the greatest of them all is love."

O God, our Father, help us so to ingraft thy words in our hearts with courage, and understand them in our minds with wisdom that we will possess both courage and wisdom for the pressing, immediate decision of our community faced with its faithlessness, of our church worried with its strength and its weakness, of our homes torn apart and pulled together, and find direction for each one of us as he turns right and turns left, as he receives and as he gives. Forgive us, O Lord, and guide us, now and always through Christ, our Lord. Amen.

13
A DIVINE ROADBLOCK

TEXT: "So Balaam rose in the morning, and saddled his ass, and went with the princes of Moab. But God's anger was kindled because he went; and the angel of the Lord took his stand in the way as his adversary. Now he was riding on the ass, and his two servants were with him. And the ass saw the angel of the Lord standing in the road, with a drawn sword in his hand; and the ass turned aside out of the road, and went into the field; and Balaam struck the ass, to turn her into the road. Then the angel of the Lord stood in a narrow path between the vineyards, with a wall on either side. And when the ass saw the angel of the Lord, she pushed against the wall, and pressed Balaam's foot against the wall; so he struck her again. Then the angel of the Lord went ahead, and stood in a narrow place, where there was no way to turn either to the right or to the left. When the ass saw the angel of the Lord, she lay down under Balaam; and Balaam's anger was kindled, and he struck the ass with the staff. Then the Lord opened the mouth of the ass, and she said to Balaam, 'What have I done to you, that you have struck me these three times?' And Balaam said to the ass, 'Because you have made sport of me. I wish I had a sword in my hand, for then I would kill you.' And the ass said to Balaam, 'Am I not your ass, upon which you have ridden all your life long to this day? Was I ever accustomed to do so to you?' And he said, 'No.'

"Then the Lord opened the eyes of Balaam, and he saw the angel of the Lord standing in the way, with his drawn sword in his hand; and he bowed his head, and fell on his face. And the angel of the Lord said to him, 'Why have you

struck your ass these three times?
Behold, I have come forth to with-
stand you, because your way is perverse before me; and the ass saw
me, and turned aside before me
these three times. If she had not
turned aside from me, surely just
now I would have slain you and
let her live.' Then Balaam said to
the angel of the Lord, 'I have
sinned, for I did not know that
thou didst stand in the road against
me. Now therefore, if it is evil
in thy sight, I will go back again.'
And the angel of the Lord said
to Balaam, 'Go with the men; but
only the word which I bid you,
that shall you speak.' So Balaam
went on with the princes of
Balak." Num. 22:21-35

William Cullen Bryant watched the figure of a wild bird
flying and floating off into the rosy depths of the sunset and
wrote some verses ending,

>He who, from zone to zone,
>Guides through the boundless sky thy
>certain flight,
>In the long way that I must tread alone,
>Will lead my steps aright.

If we really believed *that,* what conservation of our restless energy, fighting through inner conflicts and outer decisions, there would be. What harmony and creative peace would be ours if we truly believed that we rested in the will of God and could count on him always to lead our steps aright. Unfortunately, there has been so much religious nonsense about divine guidance and so much pious cant about resigning to the will of God that many of us have quite lost the sense that God can direct our ways at all. We may sing, as we have this morning, "O God, beneath thy guiding hand our exiled fathers crossed the sea" and perhaps really believe that our fathers moved beneath the Almighty's guiding hand, but for ourselves we feel little or no such protection. Rather we feel very much exposed. We must devise our own protection and figure things out pretty much for ourselves and push on the best we can with such wisdom as we can muster. This is the practical atheism by which scores of us live: ready and able to affirm the great doctrines of God but unable to believe in his ability to speak to us, to assist us in knowing and doing his will.

This primitive story of the prophet Balaam is the story of a man who, like us, tried to push through his own way and work out his own destiny without any attention to what God had in mind for him. It is also the story of a living, urgent, energetic Lord who was not dead or asleep and who had something particular in mind for Balaam and did everything he could, short of violating Balaam's freedom, to make that clear to him. If that God yet rules in the affairs of men and is the living Lord of history and of persons, of you and me, then he may speak to us today through the vehicle of this ancient and humorous story.

I

First of all, get a glimpse of this man Balaam. Perhaps we will see him more clearly all the way along if we call him Mr. Balaam or Professor Balaam or the Reverend Mr. Balaam or just plain Jack Balaam. It is clear from the story that Mr. Balaam was an honest man, the sort you might meet in church on an average Sunday—decent, hard-working, conscientious, no wife beater. He was offered an extravagant fee for doing what was questionable, and he refused it—no padded expense accounts or fur coats or deep freezers for him. Furthermore, he was apparently a gifted and talented man, at least a man with extraordinary power. Perhaps he had the power that comes with money, or the power which comes with a Ph.D., or the power that comes with a bright sparkling personality; and he was determined to employ his power in the most effective way possible. Yet, despite his honesty and his good intentions and his great gifts and his determination, he started plowing bullheadedly down a path that was displeasing to God. We do not know in what respects this action was contrary to God's will, but we do know that Balaam had managed so to insulate himself, to become so insensitive to God's will that he was blissfully unaware of the Lord's displeasure with him. When the angel of the Lord stood in his way as his adversary to stop him and turn him back from his perversity, he didn't even see him. When the Lord sent a most obvious and dramatic messenger—an angel with a drawn sword—to block his path and to turn him about, Balaam didn't see him at all and simply beat that animal all the harder and pushed on. He didn't hear or see, much less understand these obvious and dramatic messengers that came to him.

Perhaps the Lord's angel stood in his path like a blinding flash of a hydrogen bomb or like the rising and violent nationalism of an oppressed people, and Mr. Balaam turned off the car radio and pushed on the throttle a little harder. There was an important conference coming up that day and if it went well, it would mean a lot of cash. So it went three times. The Lord's angel confronted him dramatically, obviously, openly, and Balaam never saw him at all. Perhaps the second encounter was in his son's eyes when the lad said to him, "That's O.K., Pop. I don't mind going alone." And the third time may have been on his fiftieth birthday when someone said, "Well, how does it feel, Balaam, to be starting downhill?" And for a moment he wondered about that, but he quickly got hold of himself and pushed on all the harder. Three times the Lord came, dramatically, boldly; but Balaam was insulated. The flash of the bomb with the question about all humanity, and the flash in his son's eyes with the question about love, and the flash in his friend's jest with the question about life's meaning—the Lord speaking, the Lord trying to break through to Mr. Balaam—but he didn't hear.

II

And why didn't he hear? A very simple reason: he was preoccupied with transportation. Every time the angel of the Lord appeared, Balaam's steady, forward progressive movement, his going, his advancing, his motion was arrested. He was stopped, and that was all he noticed. His response was to do as he had always done, to urge the animal on. So preoccupied was he with transportation, with the *means* of getting somewhere that he resented being stopped to consider where he was going! But where are we going, and why are we

going there? Graduate school this year, Jamaica next, a good
education for the children and a therapeutic hobby and professional distinction and a party on Saturday night and raise
the church budget and paint the bathroom and publish a book
and keep on going, going, going—but why? *What is the end
of man?* Yours and mine, really? What is the purpose for
Jack Balaam, for Dr. Balaam, and Mrs. Balaam, and all the
rest of us? Well, just don't stop me right now with that kind
of question: I'm on my way to buy a new car. I know the old
one is still pretty good but—cars, ships, planes, trains, buses,
roller skates, promotions, rank, upgrade! Here we go; don't
drag your feet! Preoccupied, you see, with *means,* with transportation.

Well, that's Balaam—anxious, eager, willing, good-hearted,
hard-working, frustrated, annoyed, irritated, hurt. And when
he was stopped, his only response was just to whip the ass and
get the show on the road again. Mr. Balaam, if you please,
Doctor, Reverend, Professor, Jack and Mrs. Balaam were
well insulated from the voice of the Lord. Balaam had his
chance; he had three chances. Three times the Lord had
thrown this roadblock before him, but his preoccupation
was not altered. It was at this point that the ass he rode, however, began to speak, for Balaam was to have more than
three chances. It must be admitted that this speaking animal
did not appear as strange to the ancient Jew as it does to you
and me, for the ass was a much-honored beast, credited with
clairvoyance. However, if you are tempted to write this off
as an old legend which has no bearing on Mr. Balaam 1963,
then I beg you to consider a rather remarkable aspect of this
story, for it suggests in what follows precisely how and where
God may speak to the most stubborn, the most insulated of

us. If you have even the slightest inclination to listen for a word from the Almighty for you or for our nation, consider how the Lord did finally get through to Balaam. It may give us some important hint, but you will have to fill in the details and illustrations and examples, for they must come from your life. Here, however, are the four brief hints or clues.

III

First, the Lord got through to Balaam in a most unexpected and unorthodox fashion. Balaam wouldn't have guessed it in a hundred years. He couldn't have anticipated it. It came as a surprise in a most unexpected place. The Lord spoke, not in the temple but out in the dusty road; he spoke, not through the mouth of a priest, but through the mouth of a humble beast of burden, so that the first hint is not to limit God but to be ready to hear him even in the most unlikely places.

For example, and this is the second hint, he may speak when a long trusted and loyal servant begins to balk. "You've always served me well up to now; what's the matter with you?" We say this sometimes to our bodies when they balk, and when they balk they have a message for us and it may be a message from the Lord. Whenever those who have long loved you and served you and honored you begin to falter or oppose you—beware; it may be God.

Third, this story suggests that the God of history may be heard in the grumblings of the underdog, the oppressed, the hewers of wood, and the drawers of water. So the voice of the Almighty comes in every age to the talented and the privileged and the rich. So has it ever been! But can't you hear Mr. Balaam tell his friends that someone ought to put that animal in her place? To be sure, she has been thrown out into the field and she's been squeezed against the wall and she's been scared half to death and she hasn't been treated very kindly and she's been hit. But, nevertheless, she's got a nerve, the ungrateful thing, talking about discrimination and dissimulation! But the Lord of all Being is a God of justice and righteousness, and his voice is heard in the cries of the oppressed in every land and in every nation and in every century—from Bethlehem to Berkeley—and all our rationalization about practical matters and economic facts does not ever change eternal wrong into temporal right, and on that *we* are broken, not the Almighty. "He has scattered the proud in the imagination of their hearts, he has put down the mighty from their thrones, and exalted those of low degree."

And fourth, the Lord got through to Balaam when Balaam was completely frustrated. This should be a great comfort to some of us. You know the most wonderful humor in this whole delightful story comes to its keenest point when the ass just collapsed under Balaam. If you have had this happen to you—and some of us have had it happen quite literally —you understand the accuracy of the dictionary definition of "frustrate" as implying a rendering vain or ineffectual of all our efforts however feeble or vigorous. Well, perhaps it is only when that upon which we have counted most lies down under us and won't budge that we may listen for some word larger and stronger and lovelier than our own.

IV

Now you may wish to add to this list other hints from this story. If time were permitted we could add a word about instinct over intelligence or we would say a word about the amazing persistence of God with us; but we must move along and not miss the help this story of Balaam offers us in knowing when the Lord has got through to us.

There may be many other indications of the Lord's success with us, but Balaam's initial reaction is so often *Mr.* Balaam's reaction that it bears pointing out for it may be signal testimony to God's triumph with us: Balaam was mad; he was angry, he was hurt, he was indignant, and he was defensive. Now that's not a very happy prospect, but it often seems to work that way, and this story makes it clear. Every time the ass balks, Balaam strikes it—one, two, three— and when the ass finally complains, Balaam is indignant and defensive and angry, and he wants to lash back at it. And then he says, "You were making sport of me, you were poking fun at me. I wish I had a sword; I would kill you."

The rising anger, the indignation, the defensiveness are signs that the Lord, or if you prefer, Truth or Love or Light, is getting through our armor. When our pretensions are pierced and our soft spots exposed and our vanities uncovered and our arguments undone we react strongly, don't we, defensively and often angrily? And then, for some, the religious life, the examined life, the reflective life, the life open to God's prompting ends, ends perhaps forever, ends in fancy self-justification and rationalization. "The world has it in for me." "You can't trust anyone anyway; I'm about as good as the next, and the Church is full of hypocrites." Anger, defense, self-justification, excuses, and more unexamined life. And when that happens Mr. Balaam, even the Reverend Mr. Balaam, gets back on the animal or into the car, caught up in the grand shuttle train and goes on, preoccupied with transportation. Busy, busy, busy.

That is one way. Or the other: he stops and hears the rest of what the unexpected, balking, oppressed, instinctive, persistent beast of burden has to say and listens and considers and accepts what the Lord is saying. He hears in this annoying painful roadblock, in this irritation, in this frustration, the word of God. And then, like Balaam, confesses, "I have sinned." But that only makes sense if Mr. Balaam understands that the opposite of sin is not virtue; the opposite of sin is faith.

> He who, from zone to zone,
> Guides through the boundless sky thy
> certain flight,
> In the long way that I must tread alone,
> Will lead my steps aright.

O Eternal God, we talk to thee so much, give us the sense to stop and listen to thee. And then, if it be thy will, give the strength to do what is clear to us; especially give us the strength, O Lord, for that specific thing which we do see clearly in this moment. Through Jesus Christ, our Lord, we ask it. Amen.

14
THE SOUL'S INVISIBLE JAIL

TEXT: "And in anger his lord delivered him to the jailers, till he should pay all his debt. So also my heavenly Father will do to every one of you, if you do not forgive your brother." Matt. 18:34-35

"Ask anything of me you like, but do not ask me to forgive him. That I cannot do and that I will not do. You wouldn't suggest I should if you knew, if you really knew what I have suffered because of him. But that is not the half of it. I could forgive, perhaps, if only *I* had suffered, but look at my children or my father. How can I forgive him for what he did to them. No! That I cannot forgive and will not forgive."

So it goes. The words come easily because they are familiar. We are suddenly quiet, for we have heard them or thought them or said them ourselves. There are variations, of course, but the theme remains the same; from our own lips and from the lips of others they have sounded and they have pounded, sounding and pounding out to the same inevitable conclusion. The issue is closed. "I cannot and I will not forgive him."

Yet that is not quite the conclusion of the matter. Our text suggests that there is another line, a crucial, frightening epilogue spoken after the concluding scene. When we thought the play was over and the curtain drawn, an epilogue extending the meaning, clarifying the consequences: "And in anger his lord delivered him to the jailers."

We may withhold forgiveness if we like, and that may end the matter, draw the curtain for the one from whom our forgiveness is withheld, but it does not end the matter for us. The continuing price is great: our freedom is encircled, we are delivered to the soul's invisible jail. Invisible it may be, but crimping to the soul with increasingly little room to move about and only a slender shaft of light breaking through now and then to pierce the gloom.

I

We often say of someone jailed that he has been *arrested*. It is an apt word to describe the man who bears unforgiveness in his heart. He elects at least in some one area of his life to stop movement, growth, development. The interplay of forgiving and being forgiven is the thrust and response of growth, opening new depths of richness and poise in life, of revealing lovely, unexplored, new bypaths of mutual support and resources. Many a couple has never known how beautiful their life together could be until under the strain of a great and real grievance they have moved through the painful growth of true forgiveness. But the unforgiving man chooses a narrow little cell instead.

Thus arrested, he finds himself increasingly isolated, in solitary confinement if you will, separated from other people. The idioms of our speech describe the response he prompts in others, "keep him at arm's length," "handle him with kid gloves." So others steer their course from any real encounter with the man embittered and unforgiving, fearful they, too, will make a mistake, offend, say the wrong words—so they keep their distance. They sustain only the most superficial relationship and play it safe and thus gradually but surely the unforgiving man is isolated, jailed. He makes it clear that he lives by the rules with the quality of mercy stunted in his soul, with little patience in understanding of others' weakness and, unforgiving, he is delivered to this invisible jail of loneliness, isolated in a world of people.

For another thing this invisible jail is a place of *confinement and boredom* where the energy that might be used in creative relationships in a wide and wonderful world is turned outside in! The unforgiving man is concentrating on his own wounds, his own sorry state, nursing his old injuries, some so old they are kept infected by inward picking at the sore. He is a prisoner of self, endlessly pacing that narrow cell round and round. "The happy people," writes Dean Inge, "are those who are producing something—who are creative," but when we turn life toward self in this pitiful fashion, as we must do to keep grievances alive, there is no energy left for creating much of anything but bitterness and self-pity.

"His Lord delivered him to the jailers," and how many there are of us so sentenced by our own unforgiving determination: some sentenced for life and grimly sticking it out; others only for a year or two or thirty days, but however long, they are bleak days with soul arrested, isolated, confined. Sometimes from that narrow place we catch a glimpse through memory's benediction or in some unguarded moment of a different open world where people do live in freedom and spontaneity, even deeply wounded people who have recovered joy and peace, and when that glimpse grows clear enough, we may in desperation or in hope cry out the prayer of Mary Stuart, Queen of Scots, before her execution:

> O Master, and Maker, my hope is in thee,
> My Jesus, dear Saviour, now set my soul free
> From this hard prison, my spirit uprisen,
> Soars upward to thee.
> Thus moaning and groaning, and bending the knee,
> I adore, and implore that thou liberate me.

Then quietly the prayer may be answered, and if it is, it is answered with sure words, stern words we do not wish to hear: I cannot have mercy on you because you have no mercy on others; I cannot forgive you because your strictness, your unbending spirit is a bar locking the door through which I would come. "Should not you have had mercy on your fellow servant, as I had mercy on you? And in anger his lord delivered him to the jailers." "So also my heavenly Father will do to every one of you, *if* you do not forgive your brother from your heart."

Now this we have heard from our youth up. It is one of the clearest teachings of the New Testament. "Forgive us our debts" and then the condition of that forgiveness, "As *we* forgive our debtors!" The injunction runs all through the New Testament. "And whenever you stand praying, for-

136

give, if you have anything against any one; so that your Father also who is in heaven may forgive you your trespasses." The key to unlock the door, to liberate us from the soul's invisible jail, is our ability to forgive others. We know this teaching well, but we are bound; we seem often unable to break the chains that bind us—arrested, isolated, confined.

II

Now sermons on this theme almost always appear to be addressed to those who are simply willfully unforgiving, who make a career out of lovelessness, who find the meaning of life in keeping fresh a consuming hatred, who salt their daily bread with bitterness and season their meat from the jars they treasure filled with truculence and spite, with maliciousness and rancor. It is not boasting to say that such sermons are simply irrelevant to most of us. The more common problem is not a blunt refusal to forgive but an *inability* to forgive. The cry is not so often, "Nothing will persuade me to forgive him," but rather, "Try as I may, I just can't let my hard feelings go, I just can't forgive him. I sincerely wish I could. I know I am imprisoned by my own lovelessness, but I just can't get over the hump." Is there no saving word for the ordinary decent man who is constantly stymied in the effort to forgive? It *is* difficult, you see, for in the command to forgive, we are being asked to love our enemy—for the one against whom we have a grievance is our enemy and to forgive is to love—love our enemy: that is the most difficult thing in the world, perhaps.

This problem is not solved by the direct approach. You would think we would have learned that long ago. "There is my enemy," we say. "He slandered me; he deceived me; he corrupted my home; he stole my job; he ruined my life; or perhaps even worse, he always makes me feel the fool." At any rate, "There is my enemy, that is how I see him, that is what he is, my enemy, and now I'm just going to start loving him." What a lot of nonsense that is. As long as we hold a man in our view only as our enemy, as long as that is what he is in our eyes, that and only that, we can never love him, nor forgive him, and all the will-power, all the high resolve, all the insistent desire to do so will be of no avail. Love, forgiveness, these do not snap to attention at our command.

III

How then are we to forgive? Well, it is a step in the right direction to give up the effort to do so by the direct assault, the rigorous exertion of the will. What is needed is a new and deeper look at our enemy, a transformation of perspective, so we see in him something more and something less than an enemy. Some years ago I served as the chairman of a strenuous committee. At every session there was a member of that committee who threw cold water on every suggestion, and by his stubborn and aggressive attitude made himself generally obnoxious. He became a serious enemy, for he certainly opposed me, fought me at every turn, and made my work almost impossible. After one painful session, another member of the committee said to me, "Can't you just see him when he was a child? I bet no one would play with him, so he took to tormenting the smaller children." That comment opened my eyes, not to an obnoxious man, my enemy whom I couldn't possibly love, but to an unhappy child, emerging now as an unhappy man, who behaved as he did because of the torment he himself had experienced. Within the enemy I began to see both more and less than the enemy, a person there bruised or afraid calling forth compassion and interest and mercy; someone who could be loved and forgiven repeatedly as one who is only an enemy to us cannot be.

A contemporary writer calls our attention to a long forgotten scene in *All Quiet on the Western Front*. You may recall it. The author describes an assault in which at one point, when they came in contact with the enemy, he leaped into a shell hole. In the shell hole he found an Englishman. After the first shock of fright he considered what he should do now. Should they proceed to bayonet each other? But this bit of reflection was soon ended when he saw that the other man was severely wounded, so badly wounded that the German soldier was humanly touched by his condition. He gave him a drink from his canteen, and the man gave him a look of gratitude. The Englishman then indicated that he wanted him to open his breast pocket. He did so, and an envelope containing pictures of this man's family fell out. He obviously wanted to look at them once more. In that moment before the English soldier died, the German held up before him the pictures of his wife, his children, and his mother.

In that incident there was the revelation of another dimension to the enemy. He was not only an enemy, but he was also one who was loved and loved, who lived another life as father and husband and son. The German soldier was not prompted to have mercy on his enemy as his enemy—if he kept only that in mind, he could not love him. It was not his behavior as an enemy that provoked a warm response, but rather awareness that this man was both more and less than an enemy. That encounter provided a different way of seeing him, a transformation of perspective which revealed in his enemy that dimension of his life, potential or real, which prompted love.

We are told to pray for our enemies. We are also told that we cannot hate a man for whom we honestly pray. Doubtless that is true, but it is true because it expresses this same reality. For most assuredly when we pray for our enemy, we do not pray for what we might call his "eneminess"—that quality in him that makes him an enemy. We pray rather for him as he exists or could exist in another dimension of his life. We see the intent of God in that human creation—its denial and its potential.

Admittedly, this is difficult. In Luke, when Jesus gives the instruction to forgive always and repeatedly, the disciples respond. Increase our faith! We understand that plea! Some we cannot forgive. Increase our faith, indeed—our faith that beneath the outward distortion is the obscured but certain image of God; increase our faith so we may discern in the hardest hand raised against us the useful purpose for which God may yet use it; increase our faith to still the immediate defensive response of self and hear and speak the word God can prompt in us, of healing and of love. Increase our faith too, if we have lived so long in the soul's invisible jail that we have come rather to like it there—increase our faith to make us restless there with its barren walls and narrow ways—increase our faith to venture out. We really might be quite surprised to discover again how green is the grass, how high the hill, how warm the sun, how interesting the people, out there where men—no better and no worse than you and I—ordinary men forgive and find themselves forgiven!

Almighty God, our Father, we make bold to pray to thee because we remember thy son praying, "Forgive them; for they know not what they do," to his most direct and bitter enemies. Grant us some small portion of that grace to see through to the heart of things and find there that to which we can respond warmly and with love. Forgiving, may we know the gift of forgiveness. Through Jesus Christ, our Lord and Saviour. Amen.

15
THE GIANT KILLER

TEXT: "And David said to Saul, 'Let no
man's heart fail because of him;
your servant will go and fight with
this Philistine.' And Saul said to
David, 'You are not able to go
against this Philistine to fight with
him; for you are but a youth, and
he has been a man of war from
his youth.' But David said to Saul,
'Your servant used to keep sheep
for his father; and when there
came a lion, or a bear, and took a
lamb from the flock, I went after
him and smote him and delivered
it out of his mouth; and if he arose
against me, I caught him by his
beard, and smote him and killed
him. Your servant has killed both
lions and bears; and this uncir-
cumcised Philistine shall be one

of them, seeing he has defied the armies of the living God.'

"And David said, 'The Lord who delivered me from the paw of the lion and from the paw of the bear, will deliver me from the hand of this Philistine.' And Saul said to David, 'Go, and the Lord be with you!'

"Then Saul clothed David with his armor; he put a helmet of bronze on his head, and clothed him with a coat of mail. And David girded his sword over his armor, and he tried in vain to go, for he was not used to them. Then David said to Saul, 'I cannot go with these; for I am not used to them.' And David put them off. Then he took his staff in his hand, and chose five smooth stones from the brook, and put them in his shepherd's bag, in his wallet; his sling was in his hand, and he drew near to the Philistine.

"When the Philistine arose and came and drew near to meet David, David . . . put his hand in his bag and took out a stone, and slung it, and struck the Philistine on his forehead; the stone sank into his

forehead, and he fell on his face
to the ground.

"So David prevailed over the
Philistine with a sling and with a
stone." I Sam. 17:32-40, 48-50.

King Saul and all of Israel huddled together
in fear as day after day the Philistine giant came out from
camp on the other side of the valley and shouted his defiant
and contemptuous challenge at them, "I defy the ranks of
Israel this day; give me a man, that we may fight together."
Goliath is long since dead, but giants, fearsome and threatening, still stalk the face of the earth: hunger and poverty and
injustice filling the masses of Asia and Africa and the Amer-
icas with the power of those made mad by their own desperation; and another, a living giant, that gives their madness a
spear like a weaver's beam, a living giant spun into life by
an amoral pragmatism, these two giants abroad, man's in-
humanity and man's godlike knowledge of matter, giants with
tongues of fire long enough to encircle and scorch the whole
earth.

Goliath is long since dead, but giants, fearsome and threatening, still loom before us casting their dark shadows, not only
in the vast arena of public history, but into the quiet places
of our personal lives, too. Who knows the private, inner,
quiet giant now contending in his neighbor's heart, wanting
to rule him and destroy him: the raging of unspent desire,
the persistent joyless corroding giant of self-pity or jealousy
or the growing outline of some sickness that proposes the loss
of everything that has meant life.

It is not pleasant to speak of giants; it is not pleasant to be

144

reminded that Goliath in truth is not dead. Yet, if this ancient story is to have meaning for this day, then this painful background must be etched in first. What is it that threatens our lives, what is it that threatens your life? They are the giants we must see, acknowledge, recognize: public disease of body and of soul in Asia and Birmingham and Berkeley, bombs and educational philosophies that create intellectual wizards and moral boobs; and all the private giants coming out as Goliath did with undiminished strength at the dawn of each new day. Goliath may be dead, but his successors are persistent and his cry has not been silenced, "I defy the ranks of Israel this day; give me a man, that we may fight together."

Goliath's challenge sent Saul and all Israel shivering back into their huddle of fear, Saul and all of Israel save one unknown shepherd boy who heard the giant's threat and did not run but turned and said to the king: "Let no man's heart fail because of him; [I] will go and fight." *"Let no man's heart fail."* And the quiet courage, the rare bravery of the words stir within us that bit of the heroic which Carlyle claimed slumbers in every heart, and the pulse beats faster and our hopes are raised, hopes not about the giant, but about ourselves. Is there left within us a spark of the heroic, can we stand up to our giant and look him in the eye and be more than a match for him? Is there time, time and a bit of greatness yet within us, to face up to the worst life proposes with that intangible inner something that has set men above the beasts and close to the heart of God! Is the childhood dream yet to come true, the dream in which we saw ourselves crossing some rough water or clinging to some grand principle against wind and weather and the unthinking crowd? Is there time, time and a bit of greatness yet to face up to Goliath? Do the words of David become our words in our time to our comrades in our battles: "Let no man's heart fail because of him; [I] will go and fight"?

If you have now some public or personal Goliath clearly sketched in your mind and specifically identified, and if you feel some slight stirring again of the heroic in your soul, we are ready to move on, for the story of David offers some hints for successful strategy in overcoming giants. We have time to note only two important principles of that strategy.

I

First of all, *David finds encouragement by recalling previous experience.* Saul points out the difficulties to David, and David replied, "Your servant used to keep sheep for his father; and when there came a lion, or a bear, and took a lamb from the flock, I went after him and smote him and delivered it out of his mouth; and if he arose against me, I caught him by his beard, and smote him and killed him." David was made bold to face Goliath because David remembered other days and other dangers and other deliverances! David had a sense of history. At this moment, it was personal history. How fortunate is the youth or the man who remembers in the very shadow of a giant that he "used to keep sheep for his father," who can call up not some theory learned but some former victory experienced which buttresses his faith and quiets his fear in the hour of new crisis.

Yet, for many of us our own personal history is so unimpressive, and our own personal victories are so thin that there would be scant encouragement in recalling our own previous

146

experience. But the biblical faith takes no such isolated and individualistic view of human life. This youth who became one of the great kings of Israel relied not only upon his own experience but the experience of a people, his own people (and they are also our own people) who saw God's action in their history, a people of whom another generation would write: "And what more shall I say? For time would fail to tell of Gideon, . . . of David and Samuel and the prophets— who through faith conquered kingdoms, enforced justice, received promises, stopped the mouths of lions"; a people who continue to sense God's hand in the new covenant and in the new Jerusalem, in the Mayflower compact and with Lincoln at Gettysburg and with the slumbering Allies finally wide awake against the giant who had smashed across Europe and held Paris, the lovely lady of the Renaissance, in his crude hands.

"Religion," Emerson claimed, "is believing what the centuries say against the hours." But, alas, a person or a nation which allows the clamor of the hours with its monotonous fears and morbid pessimisms to drown out what the centuries are saying will quickly be intimidated by the giant, public or personal. A sense of history and a knowledge of it is crucial to an informed courage, yet the retiring President of the American Historical Association is alarmed, "As I see it," he recently declared, "mankind is faced with nothing short of the loss of its memory, and this memory is its history!" Frightened and dismayed is the man or nation that does not remember that "he once kept sheep for his father," that he once "conquered kingdoms, enforced justice, received promises, stopped the mouths of lions." When the teaching of history is doctored to appease the cult of Hitler or the cult of Americanism or circumvented or truncated to appease the demands of the pragmatic scientists or purged of all biblical reference to support the insane and impossible and disastrous theory of absolute separation of church and state, we cut off one of the principal resources of courage for tackling the giants who rise to destroy us both corporately and individually. Shortly after the second World War, Mr. Justice Rutledge said in an address to the American Bar Association that international law and order "can never be achieved by pessimists." I do not know what he would think about that now, but in apocalyptic times like our own, it is the voice of the centuries, not of the hours, that give rise to the only optimism that is not simply whistling in the dark. David did not whistle in the dark. His courage rested in the facts of history. He remembered that once he kept sheep for his father.

II

Note, in the second place, that *David was enabled to move against Goliath only when he declined to use Saul's armor and depended upon his own instead.* This is one of the delightful but important incidents in the story. Saul was alarmed by the determination of this young shepherd boy to meet Goliath, and when he refused to be dissuaded Saul sent for his own armor to lend the lad. The picture is clear and wonderful: "Then Saul clothed David with his armor; he put a helmet of bronze on his head, and clothed him with a coat of mail." Thus rigged up, David somehow managed to gird his sword over his armor and then the Bible reads, "He tried in vain to go." What a sight he must have been, like a little boy ordinarily fleet and fast without any shoes at all, then tripping and falling when he tries to wear his father's big ones. David was as severely hobbled and fettered and done in by Saul's armor as if Goliath himself had dropped an iron net over him. The armor was all right for Saul, but for David it was impossible.

Do we not sometimes see the Church thus hobbled in Saul's armor? On the one hand, it tries to take up the methods of comfortable society in order to win friends and presumably influence people. Its motives are as splendid as David's. It wants to move against some giant and believes that great numbers of people and a majority vote are required. So it never hints at any requirement and seldom asks any real sacrifice and takes care never to offend and a giant's net of steel could not fetter it more effectively. So it is in Eastern Europe where the communists tolerate the Church as does the conservative wing in western society so long as it refrains from any social or political judgments. It has put on Saul's armor and is fettered by it. Then on the other hand, the Church takes up the methods of a direct pressure group in society in order to win relevance and presumably be strong. Its motives again are as splendid as David's, but this, too, is Saul's armor, and in it the Church gets so involved that it begins to pontificate and to identify God's will with some particular and limited and finite scheme of man, forgetting that it, too, is subject to universal corruption; and the net of the new armor appropriate for the market place or the club or the campaign train or the political precinct immobilizes it —although it may make a good deal of noise struggling inside these coats of mail.

III

"Then David said to Saul, 'I cannot go with these; for I am not used to them.' And David put them off. Then he took his staff in his hand, and chose five smooth stones from the brook, and put them in his . . . wallet; his sling was in his hand, and he drew near to the Philistine." When at long last he put off Saul's armor and relied solely upon his own, he was ready for battle. To the casual observer or to one trained only in the methods of Saul, he was defenseless. Yet David was in truth well-armed because he was being true to himself and employing that which was particularly and peculiarly his own. So with the Church. Some years ago the cry was raised, "Let the Church be the Church!" and people who were distressed whenever the pulpit presumed to note relevance between Christian faith and economic or political matters were now relieved. They were rightly relieved *if* this slogan meant that the Christian faith does not prescribe specific schemes and remedies for the ailments of the social order; but they were wrong if they did not realize that when the Church is the Church, when it is most true to the spirit of the living Christ, when it is most deeply true to itself, its own genius and purpose, it is a vocal and ardent and persistent troublemaker and disturber of the comfortable. It must forever seek to upset the status quo whenever human beings are treated like things, or education or property or politics or economic scheme is worshiped and put before the claim of a God of love, who demands mercy and sacrifice and intelligent and reliable use of our bodies, of our property, of things; who provokes within us the love of people, people of all kinds and colors and dispositions! The armor of the Church is simple and natural and direct—sharp as a two-edged sword,

as clean as the five smooth stones from the brook, as elemental as the principle which governs the slingshot—but
powerful, especially in the testimony of the centuries against
the yakking of the hours.

And so with us, with you and with me, in our battles with
our own personal giants and our participation in the battles
against great public giants our strength is not in someone
else's armor but in relying at last on the free natural simple
armor with which God has endowed us. You remember that
mournful ballad some years back in a Broadway musical,
"How Can I Be What I Ain't!" That is only one way to look
at the problem. For many of us it is really just the opposite,
"How Can I Be What I *Am!*" We have so long tried to wear
someone else's armor, to be something that we are not, to
cover ourselves with pretense and disguise ourselves with
sophistication. How can I be what I really am? I, a single
human being, occupying a very brief and obscure place in
the whole range of human history, full of contradictions and
ailments and hindrances, yet especially endowed by my
Creator with some one talent—or five, as clean as the five
smooth stones from the brook, as elemental as the natural
laws that govern a sling—somewhere deep within me is that
which I truly am, that which is lovely and good and strong,
which is ready and able to rise and throw off much false armor,
ready to rise in elemental simplicity to overthrow the giant in
my soul and to lift the weight of my own life and my five
smooth stones against the giants who stalk the earth in our
time. "How Can I Be What I Am!" This is only found by
much prayer, by much remembering of the sheep I tended, by
throwing off armor which is not mine, in which I do not really
believe or trust and in which I hide from myself and my God,

in which I am fettered—throwing it all off and facing myself naked and honest and alone before God and finding at last his stamp in my being.

You see, if one has the courage to do that, to encounter oneself before his Maker, then—what is a giant?

O God, our time and our households call for men of courage. Give us sense to wait upon thee in penitence and in faith to receive the only armor that can encourage us. Amen.

16
PARADISE LOST

TEXT: "Eye hath not seen, nor ear heard, neither have entered into the heart of man, the things which God hath prepared for them that love him." I Cor. 2:9

Perhaps there is no Christian doctrine more embarrassing to the modern Christian who wants his religion free of any hint of superstition or wishful thinking than the doctrine of heaven, eternal life, paradise—call it what you will. He has been shown pictures of slaves working in the sweat of July singing "Swing Low, Sweet Chariot, Comin' fo' to Carry Me Home," and has been told that they were taught to believe in heaven and sing of it in order to make their miserable days tolerable, and he knows the charge has truth in it. The Marxists have moved in and chided Christians who sit in well-upholstered churches singing about Beulah Land while the world starves, and sensitive Christians have dropped the hymnbook and rushed out to pick up some share of the world's burden, deeply suspicious of their former interest in the City of God which lies beyond time and space. There are wistful tender moments when the hand of one dearly loved slips from ours, and we reach out into black emptiness trying to believe what our heart says that they cannot really be gone, that we will one day meet again, but for scores of us that faith has been corroded. We have been told that this may be wishful thinking, a groundless hope rising up for a moment to ease us through the wrenching pain only to grow thin and unsubstantial under the rough boasts of those who claim that "one world at a time" is enough for them.

However tenaciously some hope may persist of a Kingdom beyond the kingdoms of this world, we Christians have grown strangely silent about it, shamed by the many corruptions of that hope and unsure of it. Many men not quite sure that it is intellectually respectable to entertain it and unwilling to make up their minds about it have not squarely faced the issue. It strikes me that the time has come for us to confess that the hope of heaven has been misused and distorted, admit to all the perils—how it has made people indifferent to the needs of living human beings and allowed them to rationalize all manner of injustice and cruelty with pious songs about a heavenly country—admit all that but then look a little further and see what else we lose when we lose the active lively faith that "eye hath not seen, nor ear heard, neither have entered into the heart of man, the things which God hath prepared for them that love him."

At best this brief sermon can only be a very slim essay touching a small part of a question with endless complexities and ramifications, but my concern is to make clear that the classical Christian faith which affirms that this world is not the whole story is not only a matter of concern and comfort to the bereaved. It is that, certainly. We are comforted in the most profound sense of that word when we can stand here remembering our beloved dead and sing as our fathers did before us, "O blest communion, fellowship divine! We feebly struggle, they in glory shine!" To lose that comfort is to impoverish life immeasurably, and how our hearts ache for those who have been intimidated in that faith by superficial and corrupt and immoral interpretations of the Christian doctrine of heaven. But we lose far more than comfort in the face of death when we lose this dimension of faith.

I

For one thing we lose what I will call *creative poise,* the poise which enables a person to do his honest best and leave the rest to God. If we believe that this world is all there is and that our few years are all the time we have, we are apt to resemble a visitor who has five hours to spend in the Bay area and is determined to do and see everything that is worth doing and seeing. Impossible, of course, but he tries it—and if by chance in the course of the five hours he gets tied up on the Bay Bridge, he will either get out of his car and start running (that is one alternative—become a fanatic) or he will jump off into the water (that is the other alternative —complete disillusionment). The world is filled in our time with fanatics on the one hand and the disillusioned on the other! This phenomenon is especially evident in the extreme political movements of our time. If there is no fulfillment of life beyond the present experience of men, if the only value in life is dependent upon the structures and instrumentalities of human society, if it is all up to men and everything we are ever going to get we must get now—then, of course, we will become fanatics. Then when something obstructs our course, like the hump in the Bay Bridge, something we cannot do anything about directly, the fanaticism breaks out into irrational action or breaks down in disillusionment! By creative poise, I do not mean lame resignation or a do-nothing everything-is-up-to-God attitude, but the serenity which is unruffled because its ultimate confidence rests not in human success or failure, but in doing one's honest best and then being content. There is a frantic frenzied quality in life that turns our fingers into thumbs and fills our days with an awkward hectic rush full of worry and anxiety if we are in earnest about temporal life but in doubt about eternal life.

Thus when we lose faith in the completion of life beyond the present scene, we also lose the wellspring of creative poise. Belief in heaven is irresponsible escapism if we use it as an excuse to do nothing, to have no concern, for example, about earthly injustices because God will make it all right by and by! That we have clearly seen and rejected quite rightly as responsible persons, persons touched by the moral imperatives of Christian faith. But if we believe that God possesses no resources beyond those already disclosed to us here and now, then as lovers, as parents, as citizens, we will be marked either among the fanatic or the disillusioned or both, for the first usually leads to the second.

II

Not only do we lose the source of creative poise when our faith in heaven grows dim, but *we also ultimately destroy the basis for the whole Christian ethic*. When I say Christian ethic I mean the Christian fashion of treating other human beings.

156

Christian ethical behavior rests on the affirmation of the supreme importance of persons: they are made in the image of God; they are the children of God; they are loved by God. Human beings one by one have a unique status in reality. This conception is one of the fundamental contributions of Christianity to the world. The New Testament lesson today (Matt. 25) suggests that the basis of God's judgment of us is the simple test of human charity, of concern for other persons. Jesus goes so far as to say that when we attend to the needs of the hungry, the thirsty, the stranger, the naked, we are attending to him.

Many humanitarians who will have no truck whatsoever with any talk of heaven or paradise or anything which suggests the fulfillment of life beyond the grave nevertheless demonstrate a moving and sacrificial concern for persons. They hold to the Christian ethic in this regard without the Christian religion. Yet how long can they hold it? Some Oriental religious doctrines, now toyed with in certain intellectual circles, teach the reabsorption of the individual into a great impersonal spirit, and thus really deny the ultimate worth of the individual; utopian and evolutionary doctrines are content to let individuals be lost along the wayside as we march on to some fulfillment in the dim future of human history, and thus really deny the ultimate worth of individuals; and humanitarians motivated by Christian moral axioms and charitable concern but who do not believe in eternal life must consent to the apparent scrapping of individuals when the good of a greater number is at stake! If we believe that individuals really do not possess a unique and permanent status in God's eye, as the denial of heaven or its equivalent actually asserts, how long will it be before the whole Christian ethic will disintegrate! People then are means and not ends. When we deny the Christian doctrine of eternal life—however we phrase it—we are not simply turning our backs on a source of comfort in time of sorrow, but we are striking a blow at all the cultural and political arrangements which seek to secure and enhance the gift of life for persons one by one. "Take heed that ye despise not one of these little ones," but are they not in truth despised when we see a young life cut off short and can only say, "Well, that's tough!" My word, it is more than tough—if it be true that death can destroy what God creates, the importance and value of that creation is qualified, and then death, you see, is God, for it possesses the final power and has the final word.

III

My concern this morning has been to point out to someone here who is suspicious of Christian teaching about eternal life or heaven or Paradise or whatever you want to call it, that to cast it aside as a refuge for weak souls is gravely to underestimate its implications. It is not necessarily a very brave and enlightened thing to claim personal indifference to these matters, for far more is involved than our own personal desire to be released from the claim that God has on our lives. At first such indifference seems to free us; it frees us of the frightful thought of being judged or meeting God face to face—but there is much more involved than that, and we are being driven back to some of these basic considerations in our time by the lively possibility of the destruction of our neat little world with its own apparent fulfillments and conclusions.

We lose the chief source of creative poise, we lose the chief cornerstone of Christian ethics, and we also lose a sense of excitement, adventure, depth in the living of each day. To remove the dimension of eternity reduces life to a daily round, frantic for meaning in a flat surface but with no real prospect for its fulfillment.

The modern Christian embarrassed by both the imagery and the doctrine of heaven loses the lilt and the freedom and the joy of anticipating the wonder of life which is in God's hands, not his, and which takes the chill out of peril and the boxed-in feeling out of danger and the desperation out of despair. Perhaps it is this glad exultation about life, deeper than laughter and more joyous than fun which has made us suspicious of our hope of heaven—but can it be that the joy and peace which this faith at its best produces are fraudulent deceivers? If this be so, let us talk no more about order and design as witnesses to God, for in the hope of heaven disordered lives find order and distorted faces break into new designs reflecting a radiance which hints of things hidden from eye and ear but prepared by God for them that love him.

We pride ourselves, our Father, on being a practical people, trusting only that which we can see and weigh and measure and, thus, perhaps inadvertently we have lost the depth, the aura, and the mystery of life, have taken out its color and have made it flat. Grant us, we beseech thee, some encouragement to know of thy care and of realms beyond our imagination and beyond our dreams. Through Christ, our Lord.